"Oh how I love Suzie Eller's heart for prayer. It spills onto the page of this life-transforming journal. What a gift to those who struggle to find God in difficult times. This is a beautifully written, spiritually deep invitation to the joyful life you've been longing for."

Mary DeMuth, speaker and podcaster

"Struggling to find the words to chat with God? Suzie Eller's *Prayer Starters* will give you ideas for ways to start up—and continue— this most life-affirming conversation. I especially appreciate the mini Bible studies. Enjoy!"

Amy Boucher Pye, author of *7 Ways to Pray*

"If prayer has ever felt intimidating, confusing, or like one more to-do on your list, then Suzie Eller will be the gentle, wise guide you need to connect with God in ways you've always hoped for but haven't been sure how to make happen."

Holley Gerth, bestselling author, cohost of the *More Than Small Talk* podcast

"If you're like me, connecting with God in challenging seasons is hard. Suzie's book gently meets you in those places, providing God's words and creative ways to begin your conversations with God. Her biblically grounded prayers and starters come alongside you like a good friend and guide you every step of the way."

Wendy Blight, biblical content specialist, Proverbs 31 Ministries

"Suzie Eller's prayers are a gentle invitation to walk with her into the loving arms of our God—and they're so much more. They teach us how to pray. Show gratitude and humility. Reveal biblical insights. And model for us an honest, intimate relationship with Jesus. They are simply beautiful."

Kelly O'Dell Stanley, author of *Praying Upside Down*, *Designed to Pray*, and *InstaPrayer: Prayers to Share*

"Suzie Eller is a seasoned guide in those seasons that require pressing in, asking hard questions, listening in the silence, and hearing from God's heart. In *Prayer Starters*, she's taken the mystery of our prayer relationship and provided the words to begin going deeper with God, with gentleness, wisdom, and honesty."

Julie Lyles Carr, bestselling author of *Raising an Original*; speaker; host of the *AllMomDoes* podcast

"Our lungs need air. Our lives need prayer. Don't know what to say? Don't know how to pray? This book has beautiful prayers to help you start, with extra space to write from your heart, so you can learn to pray and make it a part of each day."

Amanda Hinds, founder and writer, bebraveboldstrong.com

"Prayer doesn't always come easy, especially when life's storms are raging. Suzie's *Prayer Starters* lead you into a beautiful space of prayer and worship, gently guiding you into needed prayers with God. Simply show up with an open heart and allow the prompts to spark your conversations in prayer."

Kathryn Shirey, founder and writer, prayerandpossibilities.com

"If your problems seem overwhelming, but your prayers have dried up, *Prayer Starters* is here for you! In this Scripture-soaked resource, Suzie equips you with real words for real talk with God. She's a battlefield prayer warrior who points you to the hope and divine wisdom that you need from God in your challenging times."

Barb Roose, speaker, author of *Surrendered: Letting Go and Living Like Jesus* and *Breakthrough: Finding Freedom in Christ*

PRAYER
STARTERS

Books by Suzanne Eller

*Come With Me: Discovering the Beauty
of Following Where He Leads*

*Come With Me Devotional: A Yearlong
Adventure in Following Jesus*

*JoyKeeper: 6 Truths That Change Everything
You Thought You Knew about Joy*

The Mended Heart: God's Healing for Your Broken Places

Prayer Starters: Talking with God about Hard Times

*The Spirit-Led Heart: Living a Life of Love
and Faith without Borders*

The Unburdened Heart: Finding the Freedom of Forgiveness

PRAYER STARTERS

STARTERS

TALKING WITH GOD
ABOUT HARD TIMES

SUZANNE ELLER

BETHANYHOUSE
a division of Baker Publishing Group
Minneapolis, Minnesota

© 2022 by T. Suzanne Eller

Published by Bethany House Publishers
11400 Hampshire Avenue South
Minneapolis, Minnesota 55438
www.bethanyhouse.com

Bethany House Publishers is a division of
Baker Publishing Group, Grand Rapids, Michigan

Library of Congress Cataloging-in-Publication Data
Names: Eller, T. Suzanne, author.
Title: Prayer starters : talking with God about hard times / Suzanne Eller.
Description: Minneapolis, Minnesota : Bethany House, a division of Baker
    Publishing Group, [2022]
Identifiers: LCCN 2022013991 | ISBN 9780764240232 (paperback) | ISBN
    9780764241246 (casebound) | ISBN 9781493439225 (ebook)
Subjects: LCSH: Prayer—Christianity.
Classification: LCC BV215 .E459 2022 | DDC 248.3/2—dc23/eng/20220407
LC record available at https://lccn.loc.gov/2022013991

Cover design by Brand Navigation

Baker Publishing Group publications use paper produced from sustainable forestry practices and post-consumer waste whenever possible.

22   23   24   25   26   27   28   7   6   5   4   3   2   1

Contents

PART 2 Growing in Hard Places

PART 3 Freedom in Hard Places

A Note from Suzie

Trusting God can feel fragile in hard seasons. Some of us grew up in church, and we sang the words from that classic song: *'Tis so sweet to trust in Jesus. . . .* Then circumstances or an event or a season made us question what that looks like. When we are in a difficult place—physically, emotionally, or spiritually—we may feel as if we are reaching for Jesus with all our might but aren't sure how to talk to God about what we are going through.

When I was in one of those hard and challenging seasons, I was invited to speak at an event several states away from my home. I was about to take the stage to encourage and teach other women, but the reality was I had been in an extended battle myself. My spirit was bruised. My heart was tender. Speaking to the women in that room was a privilege, but I knew the words I was about to share were for my own heart just as much as theirs.

I prayed quietly.

Lord, I need you.

A few seconds later, a woman came up to me and handed me a small bag. "I was praying for you before the event," she said. "This is for you."

Inside was a small picture of a tree with these words:

Blessed is the man who trusts in the Lord, whose trust is the Lord.
He is like a tree planted by water, that sends out its roots by the

stream, and does not fear when heat comes, for its leaves remain green, and is not anxious in the year of drought, for it does not cease to bear fruit (Jeremiah 17:7–8 ESV).

What a vivid picture! The winds whip. The heat is withering. Yet somehow the tree stands because the roots are soundly placed in the deep. That tree doesn't just make it through the drought and heat, it lives and is fruitful.

That day the Lord used a stranger to remind me of this promise:

When we are in hard times, our Source of strength is Christ.

When our roots of faith are in our relationship with him, we will one day look back to see that not only did we survive that hard place, but somehow miracles came out of those face-in-the-carpet moments.

Blessed is the [wo]man who trusts in the Lord, whose trust is the LORD.

As you talk to God every day, he meets you in the hard place. Sometimes we shy away from time with him simply because we don't know what to say. Please understand that prayer is not about the number of words that come out of your mouth. It's not about how pretty or eloquent it sounds. It's not about how loud or soft you speak. You might sit in silence, and that's okay, because God knows what you need before you even say a word.

Just show up.

As you do, your roots go a little deeper.

I'm so grateful you picked up this book. The prayer starters within are an invitation to begin the conversation you've been longing to hold with God. Each prayer starter was birthed out of a specific Scripture and is a launching pad to talk about what's been on your heart. *Prayer Starters* is a creative, interactive invitation to help you pray right where you are.

A prayer starter may lead you into meaningful conversation with God. It may create space where you just soak in his presence. It may allow you to talk with him about what has been heavy on your mind, to air your hurts, or to ask your questions. It may give you room to rejoice about things that make your heart glad. The most beautiful news is that God meets you there no matter what.

Suzie

How to Use This Prayer Book

Jesus often slipped away to talk to God. With that as our example, one of the most powerful things we can do is to create space each day to talk to him as well. That's going to look different for each of us. If there is a time that is best for you, make it a priority. If there is a place that draws you, make that your spot to meet with God (that might be in your own home or at a local coffee shop). You can carry this book with you or tuck it away in your favorite quiet place.

Find a time and place that works for you.

While there's not a best way to use this book, I'd love to share some suggestions.

- Begin with one prayer starter a day at a time. Start with the first or flip through to find what lights up your heart.
- Have a pen handy or some fun markers or colored pencils. Invite the Lord to join you as you begin (he's already there).
- Some of the prayer starters include prayer prompts. If they resonate with you, see where they take you.

- If you have more to say, and often you will, write the rest of your prayer on the page. If you have a question for him, write that down too. This is just you and God, and he loves, loves, loves you.
- If there is a day where your words are absent, let the prayer starter simply allow you to breathe in his presence. That's intimacy too.
- If you sense the Holy Spirit leading you, teaching you, offering words of comfort, hope, or even a challenge for the day, write that down.
- If you have concerns about those you love, jot those down as they come to mind. If you are like me, a hundred different things might pop into your brain—like a grocery list. Write those down and then tune back in to God.
- If you are creative and desire to color the illustrations in the book, have fun with that. This is something I love to do! My Bible and journals are filled with color and words in the margins. It's just one more way to center our hearts on what we are reading or hearing from God.
- As a prayer is answered, find the day that you prayed that prayer. Record the answered prayer and the date. This is not only a way to celebrate what God has done, but it becomes a remembrance that you can look back on one day when you need it most.

No matter how you approach this, when you intentionally seek God, you *will* find him.

That's powerful and faith changing.

If You Love to Study Scripture

While each prayer starter originates from a passage of Scripture, I share only a portion of the passage with you. If you want to combine study with your prayer time, there are several online commentary and study sites to help you do just that. A few of my favorite resources are:

- BibleStudyTools.com
- BibleHub.com
- Blueletterbible.org
- MyStudyBible.com

PART 1

Trusting God in Hard Seasons

Whatever dark tunnel we may be called upon to travel through, God has been there.

—Elisabeth Elliot

1 | You Are My Source

Heavenly Father, some days I try to make it on my own, and that doesn't work because it's in my own strength. Help me to remember that you are my Source. Your strength holds me in the winds and heat and drought. It protects my thoughts and anchors my heart. So, today I put a toe in the deeper waters of my faith. I run toward you and you alone. Though my knees are knocking and my heart is beating fast, I desire to live in the deep with you. Your presence and love will not only hold me but shine through me in ways that are surprising, even in this hard place. Help me to remember that it's not my job to do this all by myself. Thank you for taking all the pressure I've placed on my shoulders and helping me carry it. . . .

Share with God the one thing you want him to know today.

Blessed is the man who trusts in the LORD, whose trust is the LORD.

Jeremiah 17:7 ESV

2 | Help Me Remember

God, you know that faith and fear can live in the same place—in me. My fear is that this thing, this hard place, these difficulties will not end or that I'll not be big enough to make it all the way through to the other side. My faith tells me to remember who you are. You are my safe place. You set my feet on solid ground. This situation is real, but so are you. So I place this person, this thing, these feelings in your capable hands one more time, and I'll do that again and again as needed. Thank you for being my Rock. . . .

If you are carrying fear that you had put down in the past, you are not alone. Sometimes it takes a few times (or many) to put it in his hands and see it as a burden God alone can carry.

I praise God for what he has promised. I trust in God, so why should I be afraid? What can mere mortals do to me?

Psalm 56:4

3 | In This Hard Place

Father, sometimes you lead me into a harder path of faith. It takes me away from what is easy or familiar or what feels good in the moment, and I wrestle with that. I might even believe you are taking something good from me. Yet this is what I know: You have more for me. You walk in front of me on this harder path of faith. You lead and guide me every step of the way. More than that, you climb in with me. As we go through this together, I'll discover who I am—the whole me, the person you created me to be. Take my fear. Hold my hand. Lead me. I'm grateful for your mercy and grace that soak over my heart and life even in the fire. . . .

When you go through deep waters, I will be with you. When you go through rivers of difficulty, you will not drown. When you walk through the fire of oppression, you will not be burned up; the flames will not consume you.

Isaiah 43:2

4 | I Say Yes

Father, you invite me to dwell in you. Not to visit occasionally or to run to you in case of emergency. You offer refuge where I can live in you day by day, moment by moment, and all the years of my life. That secret place is hidden in my everyday relationship with you. Thank you for that beautiful invitation. I say yes to it—all of it. Today I willingly come to your sacred place of rest, shelter, wisdom, hope, encouragement, and transformation. Thank you for asking me to come as I am. . . .

Those who live in the shelter of the Most High will find rest in the shadow of the Almighty.

Psalm 91:1

5 | Nothing Misses Your Eye

Jesus, worry is often my go-to. It robs me of sleep. It chisels at my well-being. It steals the joy of today as I wring my hands about tomorrow, even when I'm not sure what tomorrow holds. Faith is a partnership with you. I show up and so do you. I take the steps that I can, and you shine a light on the next. Help me to release what I'm unable to fix or control. Help me to listen for your direction before I make my plans. Help me to let go of what is not my job or assignment. Thank you that you see every single detail and you are at work. Nothing misses your eye, including me and those I love. . . .

Worry is a thief, taking precious moments from today as you fear what might or might not happen tomorrow. Share with God one way he has met you right where you are.

Look at the birds. They don't plant or harvest or store food in barns, for your heavenly Father feeds them. And aren't you far more valuable to him than they are?

Matthew 6:26

Think on This

During our storms, you and I have the same God with us that the disciples had with them; we can trust that He is in the boat. He may or may not calm the storm immediately—we may have to endure great suffering—but He will not leave us.

—Trillia J. Newbell, *Fear and Faith*

6 | One Step at a Time

Heavenly Father, as I run this race, it feels like I may not cross the finish line. To run it well, you ask me to run moment by moment with my eyes on you. I am grateful there are thousands upon thousands of faith warriors who have already run this race. Your Word says they cheer me on as I take one step and then another. They didn't arrive at the finish line having never stumbled, and yet they crossed that finish line and you welcomed them in the end. Thank you that my prize is not the glory of the finish but the joy of running with you. If there are any weights holding me back or things you want me to hand to you so I can run this race a little lighter, show me what those are. Thank you for the roar of the crowd in heaven as I run each day, each moment toward you. . . .

Therefore, since we are surrounded by such a huge crowd of witnesses to the life of faith, let us strip off every weight that slows us down, especially the sin that so easily trips us up. And let us run with endurance the race God has set before us. We do this by keeping our eyes on Jesus, the champion who initiates and perfects our faith.

Hebrews 12:1–2

7 | I'm Really Tired, Lord

Lord, I am deeply tired. I'm worn-out in my heart, in my soul, and in my physical body. You call out to me amid my fatigue. You ask me to come to you, to find rest that syncs my heart and soul in rhythm with yours. I hold up all the things I know that have made me feel this way, and all the things I cannot even name but that you already see. Breathe rest over me, Jesus. Pour out your Holy Spirit over my tired bones. Pour your Holy Spirit over those I love and over this situation that is bigger than me. Show me physical or spiritual areas that need nurturing, even as I try to nurture everyone else. As I accept that offer of rest, slow down my thoughts and fill my heart with peace that can only come from you. . . .

What is one area where you need rest? Talk to God about that. Ask him to show you if there's one small step you can take to nurture yourself in that area.

Then Jesus said, "Come to me, all of you who are weary and carry heavy burdens, and I will give you rest."

Matthew 11:28

8 | My Strong Place

Jesus, I am tempted to lie down, to give up, and at times to throw my hands in the air and just quit. You understand this feeling because you have been tempted in all the ways I have. Thank you for that. That is why you are a strong place to bring this unwanted temptation and talk to you about it, for you not only understand it but will help me resist it. Like an invader knocking at my door in the dark hours, temptation knocks, but you answer the door. When that happens, temptation has no other choice but to turn the other way. Remind me of the true needs of my heart in this challenging place. Help me to see beyond this temporary season, this temporary battle, this temporary moment, and to settle in for the race that I'll run long-term with you. Give me the words to speak to this temptation with authority, even as I embrace all the hope and peace you give in its place. . . .

When you are tempted, he will show you a way out so that you can endure.

1 Corinthians 10:13

9 | You See

Abba Father, when I am treated unjustly you see it. You do not miss a thing. You uphold me. You hear my cries. Like a righteous lion, you are mightier than that injustice. You are greater than the evil one who desires to kill, steal, rob, and harm not just me, but those I love. Help me not to live a life of revenge in my heart but to seek justice with you as my Source. If that unjust thing happened years or weeks ago, release me to live in the beauty of today. As I sit with you in this secret place, thank you for the freedom to unburden myself of someone else's unjust actions or words, to live fully in the healing and identity you offer me. Thank you for weeping with me, for walking with me, for showing me who I am to you. . . .

We often keep these injustices buried. Bring them to the Light today. Talk to God as honestly as you can. They may be small. They may be way too big. In either case, he sits with you in your grief and loss and pain and heals your hurts.

And so at last the poor have hope, and the snapping jaws of the wicked are shut.

Job 5:16

10 | Open My Eyes

God, my eyes are on my situation, and it's all I can see some days. Expand my vision. Help me to see this through your eyes. Help me to look for you in the everyday, even in the most difficult places. Help me to see that your goodness protects and heals and intervenes when nothing else can. The battle is real, and you don't ask that I pretend that it's not. As I look to you, you help me see the small miracles unfolding all around me. You help me see those who are holding up my arms. You help me see that you not only care but are working on my behalf. I look to you, Lord. . . .

Share one need. Share one miracle you have noticed.

We do not know what to do, but we are looking to you for help.

2 Chronicles 20:12

God Is Listening

Because he bends down to listen, I will pray as long as I have breath!

Psalm 116:2

When the psalmist sang these words, he was in a desperate season, but he also found something to be thankful for during it.

God was listening to him.

There was a time Jesus was also in a desperate season. When Jesus met with his disciples for the Last Supper, he was very aware of what awaited him. In fact, it was the moment Jesus had been walking toward his whole life. He was on a mission to rescue you and me from our sins. It wouldn't be too long before Jesus would weep tears of blood, and yet he surrendered to the cross. After Jesus ate with his friends, he sang a hymn with them (see Mark 14:26).

Jesus knew what the psalmist had put into words.

Because you bend down to listen to me, Father, I will pray as long as I have breath.

God bent his ear toward both the psalmist and his Son as they talked, sang, and worshiped him. He bent his ear toward them as they cried out. In the same way, he bends his ear toward you as you talk with him today.

As you meet with God today and every day, remember that he loves you more than you can imagine and that he hears every word.

Q: In what ways does this Scripture help you as you pray?

11 | You Are My Constant, Jesus

Jesus, you are the same today, yesterday, and forever. Though it feels as if I've been up and down with all that is going on around me, I find hope in the fact that you don't change. You remain faithful. You remain close to me. You don't change your mind about your love for me, not for a second. You are still a Healer. You are my Rock. You are my foundation. When I am tempted to be swayed or knocked down by my circumstances or a word that someone spoke into my ear, those things pale in comparison to your unchanging love and strength. Help me lean into this truth and live it. . . .

Jesus is described as a Rock. He is your spiritual foundation. How does that hold you today?

Jesus Christ is the same yesterday, today, and forever.

Hebrews 13:8

12 | Secure

Holy Father, you are a deep well of peace and hope. It is why you ask me to come to you when I struggle. I am grateful that you hold out a cup of peace just for me and that you pour out hope over my heart as I sit in your presence. There is safety to be found in you. It is why I feel peace that doesn't match what I'm going through. It's why I hope when things seem dark. I need a measure of that right now. May your Holy Spirit walk with me through this day. I don't know what it holds, but I do know that with your help I will not only make it through, I will be secure and held by your power. Thank you for being a safe place to share my heart, my hopes, and my hurts. . . .

I pray that God, the source of hope, will fill you completely with joy and peace because you trust in him. Then you will overflow with confident hope through the power of the Holy Spirit.

Romans 15:13

13 | Greater than the Heavens

Heavenly Father, I am afraid because this thing I am facing is bigger than me . . . but I also know that it's not bigger than you. When you ask me not to fear, you're not saying that what I'm facing isn't big or scary or intimidating but that you are greater than the heavens and the earth, and you walk into that place or that feeling with me, and I am no longer alone. Fill me up with your strength today, Father. Cover me with your presence. Fill every nook and corner of this challenging moment. I release my fear and trust in you. I am grateful that nothing misses your eye, and you see the true need of my heart and of this situation. . . .

When you put how you feel into words, it no longer hides in the recesses of your heart; it's placed between you and God, where you can talk about it together.

Don't be afraid, for I am with you. Don't be discouraged, for I am your God. I will strengthen you and help you. I will hold you up with my victorious right hand.

Isaiah 41:10

14 | I Will Live in Truth

Jesus, there is a thief who tries to steal and rob my contentment, my peace, and my joy. Whatever this thief's plans are, your plans are so much greater for me. You came to give me life and life that is abundant—overflowing, hope-filled, adventurous, and marked by you. I reach for that full life today with all my heart. Thank you that even though my day may be challenging, it is also filled with purpose. Thank you that though my life might feel complicated, my faith is not. Lord, you are equal to every emergency and every situation. You supply all that I need (emotionally, spiritually, physically) according to your character and glory. Help me to clearly see the lies that the enemy of my soul wants me to believe, and confront them with truth. . . .

What is one truth that you will stand on today?

The thief's purpose is to steal and kill and destroy. My [Jesus'] purpose is to give them a rich and satisfying life.

John 10:10

15 | Help Me Choose My Battles

Heavenly Father, you fight on my behalf. I don't have to continually wear a set of boxing gloves but can simply let you go before me. You see the actual combat that needs to take place, and how to do that in love and might. You'll also show me how to choose my battles. You'll show me how to fight spiritually on my knees and in my heart, rather than the way I've been doing it. You'll show me how to fight for others, and also how to fight for myself in ways that are healthy and productive. Most important, you'll remind me that the battle is not mine to carry alone. . . .

This is what the LORD says: Do not be afraid! Don't be discouraged by this mighty army, for the battle is not yours, but God's.

2 Chronicles 20:15

What Are You Asking Me to Do, Lord?

If a name of a friend or even an acquaintance has come to mind this week, this is often the work of the Holy Spirit. Write that person's name down in this space.

Then, ask God to show you if there's something he wants you to do. That could be sending a text or dropping a handwritten card in the mail. It might be praying one of the prayer starters from this week and inserting his or her name in that prayer. Just remember, God isn't asking you to shoulder the responsibility of fixing anything or anyone. Instead, he's inviting you to *partner* with him because that person is deeply loved and on his heart.

- What do you sense God leading you to do?

- What might that look like?

- Share how you responded to that nudge from the Holy Spirit. Mark the date. If you return later to this page, pray for this person again.

16 | Increase My Faith

Jesus, increase my faith. As I read your Word, let the stories and verses fall into my heart like seeds. Teach me as only you can. As I talk to you, may it be with the understanding that you hear me. As I take small steps of faith, may it be with the belief that you are leading me into deep waters, and you'll meet me there. Increase my faith. Do what only you can do as I hold up what seems small to me. Multiply it and use it as you wish. I am aware of my strengths and also my weaknesses, but they are not the measure of what you can do. Help me to surrender any insecurities and trust in the security of who you are. . . .

As you begin this prayer, surrender any harsh expectations you place on yourself.

The apostles said to the Lord, "Show us how to increase our faith."

Luke 17:5

17 | When I Don't Have Words

God, sometimes when I show up to talk to you, I don't know how to describe the burden I'm carrying. I can tell you it's heavy. I can tell you that it goes to bed at night with me, and it's waiting when I wake up. Lord, you have promised a Helper. That Helper is the Holy Spirit.

Holy Spirit, you know the Father's heart and thoughts toward me. You understand the root of this burden I carry. You live inside me and are with me when I go to bed at night and wake in the morning. Even when I don't have the words to describe my struggle, you will show me how to put it down or how to work through it, with your help. I am grateful for that. Thank you for living inside me. . . .

And the Holy Spirit helps us in our weakness. For example, we don't know what God wants us to pray for. But the Holy Spirit prays for us with groanings that cannot be expressed in words.

Romans 8:26

18 | Running to You

Abba Father, I need you now. Not tomorrow. Not even an hour from now. I need you in this moment. As my daddy, God, I am grateful I can be honest about that with you. Waiting for help or hope doesn't feel like an option. Instead, I run to you. I trust you. I'm not asking you to make my circumstances go away—not in my timing at least—but to make yourself present during them. You are not far from me. You are real and you are everything I need. I climb into the refuge you offer. I anchor my heart and thoughts in you. Thank you that in this moment you hear my cry for help. . . .

O God, don't stay away. My God, please hurry to help me.

Psalm 71:12

19 | Shine through Me

Heavenly Father, I feel like a clay vessel—so very ordinary and fragile. Yet the ordinary is where you shine the greatest. Your brilliance shines through the cracks in the darkest of nights. Others see a clay pot and they know that what is revealed is real, for the ordinariness of such a vessel cannot do this on its own. You are the Potter, God. Shine through me. Filter through the cracks and let the beauty of your presence draw others to your love. Create hope in their hearts if they are without it. May those who don't know you wonder how such joy or peace is possible. Though I am ordinary, you are extraordinary, and I invite you into every part of who I am, right where I am, so that you may shine brightly in ways that draw others to you. . . .

Even when we are in the darkest night, Jesus still shines through the cracks. Your faith is luminous right now, and that is a beautiful thing.

And yet, O Lord, you are our Father. We are the clay, and you are the potter. We all are formed by your hand.

Isaiah 64:8

20 | Open Hands

Jesus, as you walk through this with me, I feel there is something you are trying to give me. There are reasons I struggle with receiving it. I may feel unworthy some days. I may think about all the other people who need you or may compare my situation with theirs and find their hurt greater. I may struggle to receive your kindness and presence—and yet the truth is I desperately need what you are offering. Thank you for not giving up on me despite my resistance. Thank you for meeting my objections with the truth that I am not supposed to do this alone. I will receive what you are trying to give with open hands. I accept all of it. I need you not just today, but every day and in every way. . . .

Simon Peter exclaimed, "Then wash my hands and head as well, Lord, not just my feet!"

John 13:9

Hey, Friend, Just So You Know . . .

I began realizing it was okay to just sit with Him. It was okay to just be still. It was possible to find Him in the immense stillness, the hidden parts of my heart. He was always there in my hiddenness.

—Natalie Brenner, *This Undeserved Life*

Q: What is one way that you can be still today?

21 | You Are My Stronghold

Lord, you are my stronghold in the day of trouble. I find protection in the fortress created from your love. Thank you that what I'm facing is not a lifetime of trouble after trouble, but a moment, a day, a temporary season that will one day be a distant memory. I'm grateful that when I approach your fortress of love, you throw open the door and welcome me in. There I find everything I need—a place to rest, refreshment from the inside out, hope that is not based on my situation, and strength that will hold me. You know about the battle raging outside the fortress. Nothing about this battle surprises you, but you also know what awaits me inside. I will sit in this fortress of love for as long as I need, for you know the thoughts of my heart, both brave and not so brave, and will love me well through both. . . .

You may not feel brave today, but running to him is not only brave, it is wise on your part. Imagine a fortress carved out of God's love. Step inside. Take a deep breath. Talk to him.

The LORD is good, a strong refuge when trouble comes. He is close to those who trust in him.

Nahum 1:7

22 | Yes to That Miracle

Savior, when problems seem as high as the highest mountain, you see them from a different vantage point. You see every peak, but you also see how that mountain will change me as I climb it. You promise surprising miracles as I scale its heights. Perhaps the miracle is that I'll see things that I can't any other way. Maybe that miracle will take place in the heart of a loved one or in a situation as they see you walking with me. Perhaps the miracle will be one of trust. Instead of trying to do more on my part, I'll take rests along the way as you lead, because that is also a miracle. In the rest, you take my eyes off the mountain long enough to place my hand in yours, so we can climb it together. . . .

"For the mountains may move and the hills disappear, but even then my faithful love for you will remain. My covenant of blessing will never be broken," says the LORD, who has mercy on you.

Isaiah 54:10

23 | Deep and Wide

Jesus, the love you have for me is deep and wide, and it's hard to fathom at times. It's a love that marched toward a cross willingly. It's a love that wrangled with the enemy of our souls and marched out victorious. It's a love that battled death, hell, and the grave so that I might have life. This is the love you have for me, and for the world. It is also the love you have for the one I care about—the one I love who has lost their way. Your love is high, wide, deep, even as [*insert your own name or another*] seems to be miles outside your plan. Your love is high, wide, deep, even as [*insert your own name or another*] isn't always sure how to turn to you. Today I embrace this unfathomable love for my own soul, and I ask that [*insert their name*] be swept away by it as well. I pray [*insert their name*] senses that love wherever they are. . . .

And may you have the power to understand, as all God's people should, how wide, how long, how high, and how deep his love is.

Ephesians 3:18

24 | This Is Who You Are

God, O God, all-powerful, all-knowing, and my Abba Father, these are not just your names. These are who you are. Thank you for the wisdom of godly people. Thank you for those who are kind. Thank you for those who don't know what to say but show up anyway. Thank you for wise counsel. These are all good gifts, and I am grateful. Most of all, I want to thank you that you do what people cannot. You see beyond the obvious to the need inside. You peel away layers so that I find the person you created me to be. You see my flaws, but also what makes me strong. Heal me, Lord, and I will be healed; save me and I will be saved, for you are the one I praise. . . .

As you talk with God today, let it be with the knowledge that he knows what you need before you even say one word.

O Lord, if you heal me, I will be truly healed; if you save me, I will be truly saved. My praises are for you alone!

Jeremiah 17:14

25 | Where Would I Go?

O Jesus, I know what it is to feel far from you. I know what it is to want to give up. Yet where would I go, except for you? Thank you that when I feel this way and I call out to you to restore the joy of my salvation, you hear me. It is your delight to remind me why I call myself yours, and why you call me your child. While obedience is good, what you want is connection. That is what changes my heart. That is what draws me back to you. Restore to me the joy of my salvation. . . .

Don't confuse being battle weary with sin. Obedience isn't about following a rule. It's surrender. Surrender today to the goodness he has for you.

Restore to me the joy of your salvation, and make me willing to obey you.

Psalm 51:12

What Is So Different about Them?

Ordinary . . .

That's what the authorities said about the early disciples in Acts 4:13. These believers didn't have multiple degrees or pedigrees. Some worked with their hands from sunup to sundown. Yet there was something special about these ordinary, unschooled believers.

They had been with Jesus.

Was that it?

It was.

In the darkness that you are in right now, the Light within you flickers. You are pressed down, shaken, embattled, and yet you reach for Jesus. Those on the outside wonder:

How is she okay?

What is different about her?

The world can't help but note, my sweet friend, that you have been with Jesus—even in the hard places, especially in the hard places. It's not about how resilient you are in your own right. It's a deep-rooted, she-belongs-to-Jesus light that burns brightly right where you are, and that is beautiful.

26 | I Am Seen

Clothe me, Lord, in dignity and strength. Not for show. Not to appear a certain way. Clothe me with dignity and strength so that I am sheltered by these things and so that I may offer shelter for others. I know who I am to you. I am loved. I am treasured by you. You see me. This sense of self comes from a Savior pouring his love over my heart. It's identifying as yours. Thank you for strength that covers me in any storm and shines a light so others can come in from the storm too. Thank you for surprising joy, for laughter that is deep and authentic, and for your covering in both good and difficult times. . . .

The word dignity can feel stiff or formal. In today's passage, it's neither of those things. It's simply knowing whose you are and wearing that identity. You are stronger than you know.

She is clothed with strength and dignity, and she laughs without fear of the future.

Proverbs 31:25

27 | Help Me Hear You

Father, you shut the mouths of hungry lions. You stood against evil with justice and might, time and time again. I love that about you, for this means I do not have to live in fear, for I am yours and you fight for me. You are not unaware or uncaring but stand against all the roaring lions. Father, shut the mouth of the lion in my life in whatever form it tries to come. May the only roar I hear be the words of your promises and truth over my heart and life. . . .

Name that lion. Hear his roar diminish as he sees who stands with you. Write down one truth the Holy Spirit has spoken over your heart, either today or in the past.

Then Daniel spoke to the king, "O king, live forever! My God sent his angel and shut the lions' mouths. . . ."

Daniel 6:21–22 ESV

28 | On Every Day

Jesus, today I will take a deep breath and rest in your competence. Some days I'm a mess. Some days I have it together. Some days it looks like I'm doing all the right things, but I'm crumbling on the inside. In each, I am grateful that it's not all dependent on me. My confidence is in you. It's found in your unchanging character. It's found in your promises that, once stated, don't go away. It's found in the truth that you live in me—and that means that wherever I am, whatever I'm facing, however I feel on that day or in that moment, you are near and are capable of leading me, teaching me, comforting me, launching me, and loving me. I receive all of that today, beginning with this one thing. . . .

We are confident of all this because of our great trust in God through Christ.

2 Corinthians 3:4

29 | Hold My Tears

Jesus, I can't deny that I am in a troublesome season. It feels as if hardship is coming from every side. Yet you are close. Thank you that you offer me an untroubled heart even in troubled times. From the outside looking in, that may seem impossible, but I know it's possible in you. Help me to place my trust in you in this moment to find what my heart needs. Hold my tears in your hands. Guide my feet and my choices. When I lay my head to rest, may it be with the assurance that you were with me in every part of this day. I hold up every troublesome thought, every troublesome circumstance, and I receive your love, which soothes my troubled heart, and your guidance, which shows me what to do. . . .

Don't let your hearts be troubled. Trust in God, and trust also in me.

John 14:1

30 | You Make Me Brave

Heavenly Father, you don't just offer sympathy. You offer comfort. You reinforce me. You assist me. You make me brave in ways that surprise me. I know this comes from you. I am grateful for those who have come around me in this hard place and shared their stories. They know what it is to feel lost or overwhelmed, and yet they made it to the other side. I may not be able to share my full story yet, but I thank you that what I'm going through today will one day help someone else find their way to you. That is only one of the miracles you will do through this difficult time. . . .

Perhaps you'd like to talk to God about one miracle or one way he has comforted you.

He comforts us in all our troubles so that we can comfort others. When they are troubled, we will be able to give them the same comfort God has given us.

2 Corinthians 1:4

Write It Down. Make It Plain.

In several places throughout God's Word, people are instructed to write down what God is doing (Habakkuk 2:2; Revelation 1:19; Jeremiah 30:2; Romans 15:4; and others). These words became history, but also *her* story.

Through one person's journey, that God story was revealed to generations to come.

There is history unfolding as you trust God in these more difficult paths. While the more obvious storyline might be loss, pain, unwanted circumstances, or opposition, there is an underlying story of trust, leaning into Someone greater, growth, comfort, endurance, and more.

The reality is that one day this will be only a part of your overall story.

Share the battle that you are in. Write it down. Make it plain.

One day you'll look back and read your own words, and it will not just be history, but it will be *her* story.

Your story.

Those words will be a reminder of who God is, and what he did, and those small and big moments that carried you through. They will serve as a reminder of God's faithfulness and love. And perhaps they will even become a marker for someone else of God's faithfulness.

Q: What is one thing God has done in you, or for you, or through others in the past thirty days, big or small? *Write it down. Make it plain.*

PART 2

Growing in Hard Places

For the Lord is the Spirit, and wherever the Spirit of the Lord is, there is freedom.

2 Corinthians 3:17

31 | You Know Me

Jesus, I understand the futility of trying to stand against suffering and hardship in my own strength, but asking for help is hard. You know that about me. Yet I need you. Oh, how I need you, Jesus. That is my cry. I need you in my sweetest of moments. I need you when I am dancing in celebration. I need you in my closest relationships. I need you when those same people hurt my heart. I need you as I forgive them and as I forgive myself for falling short. I need you when my back is pressed against the wall. I acknowledge that I need you in all these moments. I am grateful that as I express that need, you settle my heart. . . .

Our God loves to do life with us both in the good and the difficult places. Invite him to join you right where you are today. Tell him about one good thing and one hard thing you are experiencing.

In his kindness God called you to share in his eternal glory by means of Christ Jesus. So after you have suffered a little while, he will restore, support, and strengthen you, and he will place you on a firm foundation.

1 Peter 5:10

32 | Draw Me to Truth

Father, I am a field waiting to grow. Your Word in my heart creates roots to hold me in any season, but especially in this one. Take that seed of encouragement and truth found in your Word and bury it in my heart. I am grateful your Holy Spirit brings it to life—sometimes right there on the page, and other times it comes to me when I need it most. There are a lot of things competing for my attention, and you see and understand that, but you also draw me to your Word. Help me not only to seek the Word on my own but to find and become a part of a community that will help me grow in the Word. I hold up my mind, my soul, my life, and I am open to every beautiful seed you desire to establish in me. . . .

And the seeds that fell on the good soil represent honest, good-hearted people who hear God's word, cling to it, and patiently produce a huge harvest.

Luke 8:15

33 | I Have a Helper

Holy Spirit, enlarge my understanding of the character of God so that I might trust you more. Increase my knowledge of Scripture so that I might fight bravely with its truth and walk in its wisdom. Show me what you see when things are murky, rather than my shortsighted view of my circumstances. Speak over my heart when I need to pause or stop completely. Give me the courage to follow through when you give the green light. I am thankful that I have a Helper in you—for you know the heart of Father God and your plans for me, and live right inside of me. . . .

You have a Helper. In what ways do you need his help? Ask for it.

We ask God to give you complete knowledge of his will and to give you spiritual wisdom and understanding.

Colossians 1:9

34 | Complete

Heavenly Father, you have never left anything half-finished. You created the world in all its beauty and said, "It is good." You sent Jesus to do a work on my behalf and you called it complete. You refuse to leave anything half-formed or half-finished, and that includes me and your plans over my life and those I love. I may not always understand all the pieces of your plan, but I believe they will fall into place in your timing. I surrender all that I am to you, trusting in your final plans and your timeline. . . .

We often think that the completed work is the masterpiece, while every facet of the plan is integral to the final work. What is one way God is creating a masterpiece inside you right where you are?

And I am certain that God, who began the good work within you, will continue his work until it is finally finished on the day when Christ Jesus returns.

Philippians 1:6

35 | My Part in Your Plan

Father, there's a seat for me in your kingdom and in your work, even now. I'm a part of your plan to love the world, and that hasn't changed. What you are asking me to do might not look like someone else's role, but it's absolutely for me. Just because I'm going through difficult times doesn't mean I'm not part of your plan. My story might resonate with one person and help him or her feel like they are not the only one going through that situation or feeling that way. My talents might look different from others, but they are just as valuable when they are used by you. Thank you that you call all of us to work together and to make a difference in the world with your love and with the Gospel. Thank you for the opportunity to partner with you to love the world. . . .

Scripture shows that God is often revealed most powerfully in the pit, the lion's den, and even in prison. Open your heart to whatever work he longs to do in or through you.

When I think of all this, I, Paul, a prisoner of Christ Jesus for the benefit of you Gentiles . . .

Ephesians 3:1

A Mantra of Hope

A *mantra* is a saying that you speak over your own heart as truth. It becomes a banner of sorts, as you speak it out loud when you need it most. Read this mantra of hope out loud. Underline anything that speaks to your heart in this moment.

Though I don't understand fully why I am in this place, I am not alone.

Though I feel the burden of this moment, I do not carry it by myself.

Though my tears fall freely, so does the love of my Savior wrap around me.

Though I am not sure of the next step, the Holy Spirit will shine a light on my path.

Though I feel my plans have been sidetracked, God's plans for me remain.

Though I feel weak, my power is found in his.

Q: What is one more line you may want to add to this mantra to make it your own?

Though I . . .

36 | Break Down Those Walls

Lord, when I gather with others to pray, your presence settles. Suddenly the fight looks different. While one can battle for a round, a team can fight all the way to the end. One steps in when another is weary. Another steps in when it feels too big. Help me to break down any walls that I've built around my heart when it comes to your people. Help me to see humans as both strong and fallible, just like me. If a measure of grace is needed, help me scoop from the vast grace you've given me. Remind me to share my needs, rather than expecting people to guess. Take my eyes off the one who didn't show up, and help me to appreciate those who did. There's power in connection and community, Jesus. . . .

What do you long for in a community? Pray for that.

For where two or three gather together as my followers, I am there among them.

Matthew 18:20

37 | In the Heart of the Storm

Savior, I know you ask me to trust you, and I do. Yet there are days that all I can see is the reality of the storm. I feel it. I want it to end. So, I run to you again, knowing that you aren't worried about me disturbing you with my fears, and that you care about how those fears disturb me. You will speak to the storm on my behalf—especially the one raging inside me. Speak to the fear that tries to capsize me. Remind me of the peace you feel and help me to remember that same peace is for me too. You have authority, and you offer me, as your daughter, the same authority to speak to the winds and waves. Ah, thank you, Jesus. I'm sitting close with you now to share my fear with you and to embrace the calm you long to give. . . .

The disciples were amazed. "Who is this man?" they asked. "Even the winds and waves obey him!"

Matthew 8:27

38 | You Fight *for* Me

Abba Father, justice is in your hands. This doesn't mean there isn't a part for me to play, but it's not my job to live my life making someone pay for their wrongs. It's exhausting. It attempts to consume me when there are sweet and better things you have in store for me. You ask me not to fret—worry, fuss, agonize—over those wrongdoings, but to rest in you. You reassure me that you are a God of justice, and this injustice has not escaped your attention. You are not callous to the damage it has caused. Yet you also offer comfort and healing in abundance. You summon me to freedom from those things I cannot fix. You remind me that their brokenness is not my identity. Today I release the space in my heart dedicated to that wrongdoing, so that I can laugh and love and live again. . . .

Be still in the presence of the LORD, and wait patiently for him to act. Don't worry about evil people who prosper or fret about their wicked schemes.

Psalm 37:7

39 | Seed Sower

Father, I'm so thankful you don't define success in the same way that the world does. It's not about being good in our own right. It's not about how much I have here on earth. You simply call me to plant seeds. I can plant a seed of encouragement in someone's heart. I can plant a seed of laughter in a moment that needs it. I can plant a seed of hope where hope feels far away. Those seeds flourish right where they drop, in the strangest of places and in the most incredible ways. When I look back one day, I won't just see this as a difficult time but as a series of days in which you still allowed me to be a seed sower. As I go through this day, may a seed fall from my relationship with you and take root where it's needed. . . .

So let's not get tired of doing what is good. At just the right time we will reap a harvest of blessing if we don't give up.

Galatians 6:9

40 | On My Knees

Father God, it's so easy to see that person or that thing as my enemy. I put on my boxing gloves and swing wildly until my arms can swing no more. Help me to fight where it's most effective—on my knees and in your presence. Not in my own power, but in yours. Help me to stand in your authority, knowing that you go before me. Crush every plan of the enemy with your might. If I need others to join me in prayer, give me the wisdom to reach out and share that with other prayer warriors. Most of all, thank you that you are higher, greater, more powerful, and that you fight for me daily. . . .

What do you need today? Clarify it for yourself. It's okay if it's raw. Try to put it in words.

For we are not fighting against flesh-and-blood enemies, but against evil rulers and authorities of the unseen world, against mighty powers in this dark world, and against evil spirits in the heavenly places.

Ephesians 6:12

When You Are Afraid

As evening came, Jesus said to his disciples, "Let's cross to the other side of the lake." So they took Jesus in the boat and started out, leaving the crowds behind (although other boats followed). But soon a fierce storm came up. High waves were breaking into the boat, and it began to fill with water. Jesus was sleeping at the back of the boat with his head on a cushion. The disciples woke him up, shouting, "Teacher, don't you care that we're going to drown?" When Jesus woke up, he rebuked the wind and said to the waves, "Silence! Be still!" Suddenly the wind stopped, and there was a great calm. Then he asked them, "Why are you afraid? Do you still have no faith?" The disciples were absolutely terrified. "Who is this man?" they asked each other. "Even the wind and waves obey him!"

Mark 4:35–41

Have you ever seen a toddler try to stay awake when they are tired?

Little legs dangling from the couch, soft snores from their lips. Asleep in the high chair, spaghetti in their hair. Sleeping peacefully in church, regardless of the booming music coming from the stage.

Jesus was in the hull of the boat sleeping like a *baby*. How else can you describe a man fast asleep in a rocking, thrashing boat? The disciples were aware of the long day Jesus had just experienced. He had prayed for people from sunup to sundown.

They didn't want to wake him—until they had no other choice.

When it seemed that the boat might capsize, they called his name in a panic and rustled him awake. Jesus rose and took in the dark skies and rolling clouds. Water splashed his face. He took in the sight of the loyal disciples who followed him. Many of them were lifelong fishermen. For them to be afraid meant it was a significant squall, one that could potentially toss them all into the depths of the lake.

Jesus spoke . . .

He replied, "You of little faith, why are you so afraid?" Then he got up and rebuked the winds and the waves, and it was completely calm (Matthew 8:26 NIV).

Some read this story in the book of Matthew, and they believe that Jesus is angry with the disciples. Other theologians picture a different scene. Jesus asked a question of the disciples, but his rebuke was for the winds and waves. Even before he addressed the storm, he focused on the tempest inside his friends. He knew of their faith. He also understood their humanity. With one humble question, Jesus was reminding the disciples of what they already knew.

Remember who you are.

Remember the miracles you saw earlier today.

Remember who I am.

It was a centering of sorts, helping them find their way to peace.

Once his friends were calmed, he tackled the storm.

Tone it down.

And the winds and waves obeyed.

When the waves feel way too high

Are you in a raging storm? Maybe you thought you had it under control. After all, you've done this before, but this new storm seems overwhelming.

Call his name.

It may feel like he's asleep, but he's not unaware. He sees the storm from a vast perspective, one that includes the past, present, and future. He sees your fear, but he also knows your faith. He is not mad at you because you panicked or felt uncertain. He loves, loves, loves you. Tell him what is on your mind.

Let him remind you of who he is, and who you are. Let him calm your heart.

Let him speak to the storm and calm the waves.
Take a moment and talk to God about that now.

_____

_____

_____

_____

41 | Meet Me in the Fire

Heavenly Father, you don't throw me into the fire. Instead, you meet me in the fire. That's how it's possible that I make it through. It is in the fire that I discover you are real. It is in the fire that I turn to you and find comfort, courage, and direction. It is in the fire that you teach me how to endure. My faith grows, not because of this fiery trial, but because I discover who you are despite what I'm going through. Lord, trials like this test my faith, but you always pass the test, and that holds me tight. Thank you for meeting me in the fire. . . .

What is one way your faith is holding you in this trial?

_____

_____

_____

_____

_____

_____

So let it grow, for when your endurance is fully developed, you will be perfect and complete, needing nothing.

James 1:4

42 | Holding Fast to You

Jesus, when discouragement comes, help me to meet it with honesty. You are a secure place to share how I feel. When temptation wags its finger, help me to remember that you have suffered every temptation. You not only understand that temptation but will overcome temptation with truth and authority, giving me what I need to move past it. Help me to be steadfast and unmovable. Help me to lean into your truth. Remind me to hold fast to you. To dig into your Word, for your Word is a weapon that protects my heart from the one who desires to shake my faith. Thank you that, in a world that feels unpredictable, you are unchanging. Wrap me in your glorious power today, and thank you for giving me what I need. . . .

We also pray that you will be strengthened with all his glorious power so you will have all the endurance and patience you need. May you be filled with joy.

Colossians 1:11

43 | Not Just Me, but Me *and* You

Abba Father, if I were to make a list of all the times you have provided for me, that list would be long. At some point my faith moved from "church" to a relationship between you and me. That is everything! You provided wisdom. You provided help. There were times I thought I was at the end of my rope, and you provided just enough hope to hang on. I'm reaching out to you from the heart of that relationship one more time. Help me to find contentment in this season, not in what I have or what I do, but in us. . . .

God loves you like crazy. Ask for strength that springs from your connection with God.

For I can do everything through Christ, who gives me strength.

Philippians 4:13

44 | In the Wilderness

Father, no one wants to be in the wilderness, and yet I've been there for a while. I know it's not my forever home, but it's where I am and I'm ready to move on. Meet me in this wild place. Settle over me at night while I rest. Be my protection as you keep me safe in heart and mind. I know this trial isn't an eternal part of my life. The forever part is you. You are with me in the wilderness, on the mountaintop, in the valley, and in every season and in every moment. Keep my heart, reinforce my faith, and may my love for you run wild and deep today and every day. . . .

Invite the Lord to join you in the wilderness. Share with him the protection you need.

David now stayed in the strongholds of the wilderness and in the hill country of Ziph. Saul hunted him day after day, but God didn't let Saul find him.

1 Samuel 23:14

45 | I Am Hurting

Jesus, I am hard-pressed. I am perplexed. I am suffering. But I am also not broken. I am not forsaken. I am not overlooked. Thank you that you understand my suffering—for you walked a path you didn't ask to walk, yet somehow your suffering brought about victory and confounded the enemy. You spoke the Word in your suffering and your glory was revealed. Though I am not you, I am yours, and I hold up my suffering to you. Step into it with me. Use this for your glory. May I one day look back and see how your nail-scarred hands and your battle-scarred heart held and protected and warred for me and how victory was won over and over again. . . .

Your Savior finds no joy in the fact that you are suffering. He understands the battle. He also sees down the road. Hold up your hand to take his nail-scarred hand in yours.

We now have this light shining in our hearts, but we ourselves are like fragile clay jars containing this great treasure. This makes it clear that our great power is from God, not from ourselves.

2 Corinthians 4:7

The Beauty of Battle Scars

Richard pulled a T-shirt over his head. As he did, I couldn't help but see the scar angling down the center of his chest. It came out of a day I'll never forget. We had walked five miles the night before. He was a runner, ate healthy, and had no underlying health issues—and yet he called me as he raced toward the emergency room.

We almost lost him that day.

It took weeks of recovery, but he got stronger.

Our grandchildren were fascinated by that long, jagged scar on his chest, deciding such a grand scar needed a tattoo.

Maybe a unicorn horn or a sword.

The intimacy of seeing each other's scars

When Richard and I first married so many years ago, we had no idea that life would leave such marks. I battled breast cancer at a young age, and again recently. He bears scars from the heart attack and open-heart surgery.

Just the act of living leaves a nick here, a scar there on all of us.

There's intimacy as we reveal our scars. Some on the outside. Some inside. We recognize we've all been in battles, and yet we made it to the other side. Perhaps that's why I love the story of Jesus showing his scars to Thomas.

Let's look at that passage together.

Eight days later, his disciples were again in the room. This time Thomas was with them. Jesus came through the locked doors, stood among them, and said, "Peace to you." Then he focused his attention on Thomas. "Take your finger and examine my hands. Take your hand and stick it in my side. Don't be unbelieving. Believe." Thomas said, "My Master! My God!"

John 20:26–28 MSG

Thomas was away the first time Jesus appeared to his disciples. When he arrived, his friends rushed to tell him what had taken place. They had seen Jesus! He talked to them.

Thomas struggled to believe it, and why wouldn't he?

He had seen Jesus' broken body on the cross. He witnessed the sealed tomb. Perhaps he reasoned that his friends were under duress. Perhaps they were delusional.

Maybe they were jesting.

Eight days later, Thomas was in the room when Jesus made a second appearance. Jesus' focus was on Thomas. He went straight to him, inviting Thomas to touch his scars.

Why did he do this?

Perhaps it was because Thomas had his own scars that day. Inner wounds still raw and tender. Those wounds were inflicted in the days leading up to Jesus' death. They came from upheaval. There were wounds of uncertainty. Thomas thought he knew which way life was going until it all fell apart. As Thomas placed his hand on Jesus' scars, they told a story.

This scar represents your freedom to walk into the powerful presence of God. No more sacrifices or rituals needed. Just come on in.

This scar represents cleansing from all sin. Not just your sin but the sin of the whole world.

This scar represents powerful peace. I bore it upon my own body, Thomas. It's for you.

This scar represents healing. Healing from physical, spiritual, emotional wounds.

This scar represents the sorrow I took upon my shoulders, so that you might experience renewed joy.

As Thomas witnessed Jesus' scars for himself, he didn't see death or a tomb.

He saw life.

He didn't see jagged edges of healed wounds.

He saw how far Jesus went to rescue him.

"My Master! My God!" he cried.

Something miraculous happened in that moment. Everything Jesus had ever spoken to Thomas was true. He understood that now.

Jesus' scars brought healing to Thomas.

Perhaps you feel scarred from the inside out.

Our inner scars come from a myriad of sources. Unwanted news. Things you didn't want to go through. Emotional valleys you'd have rather skipped. Times you wondered what in the world was happening.

Whatever those scars look like, Jesus understands what they represent.

He knows the pain and suffering that brought those scars to life.

There's intimacy as you show him your scars and tell him your story. There's intimacy as you accept his encouragement to come a little closer and see the scars he bears on our behalf.

Those scars represent healing for you, inside and out.

- Tell Jesus about one of your scars, past or present.

- Read Isaiah 53:4–6. Imagine, like Thomas, you are placing a hand on one of the scars represented in this passage. What does that scar represent to you?

46 | Light Me Up

Jesus, darkness cannot remain where you live, and you live in me. That means light lives in me, even in the dark night. As I look to that light today, I find you as the Source. You will help me find my way, even if I can't see two inches in front of me. You will guide me as I make difficult decisions. You blaze a light of hope. When darkness dares to try to close in on me, you are greater. . . .

Your feet are secure even in the dark, for he illuminates the way. Ask for the Light you need.

Jesus spoke to the people once more and said, "I am the light of the world. . . ."

John 8:12

47 | Change the Way I See Things

Jesus, open the eyes of my heart to see the way you do. Enlighten me. Inform me. Instruct me. Teach me. Peel back the curtain so that I can see the whole picture—the one where you are over the whole world, and yet notice the sparrow. The one where you created the earth and all that is in it yet know the exact number of hairs on my head. The one where you envision the hope of my calling in all seasons, not just when things are the way I want them to be. Open the eyes of my heart, Lord. Seeing through your lens has the power to change everything. It has the power to change me. . . .

I pray that your hearts will be flooded with light so that you can understand the confident hope he has given to those he called—his holy people who are his rich and glorious inheritance.

Ephesians 1:18

48 | A Deep Soaking

God, when I am poor in spirit, it doesn't mean I'm without hope. It simply describes the gap between what I need and what you hold out to me. Today I need joy. Joy that is hidden within me, buried like a seed, and watered by you. This joy, when it launches, is untouchable. It's separate from what is outside of me and rests in you as its Source. It cannot be taken from me, for it is rooted so deeply that external circumstances only ripple the surface. Pour out your joy in abundance and splash that joy on those around me. . . .

A biblical definition of joy is "intentionally walking into the goodness of God." Don't be afraid to share your need for a joy that comes from the inside out with the Source of joy.

Blessed are the poor in spirit, for theirs is the kingdom of heaven.

Matthew 5:3 ESV

49 | You Are Compassion

Jesus, when you walked on earth, you noticed those who were hungry. You didn't walk past the leper. You knelt with the woman caught in her sin. What I love most about this is that you didn't leave them there. You gave them bread. You touched the skin of one scorned for his disease and made him whole. You looked into the eyes of a woman who had lost all hope and gave her a new beginning. You are not just my God of compassion; you *are* compassion. You don't just preach an idle message; you *are* the message. Just as you noticed each of these, I take comfort that you have noticed me too. You not only notice me, but you also know what I need. Thank you for stopping to be with me today. . . .

Then Jesus called his disciples and told them, "I feel sorry for these people. They have been here with me for three days, and they have nothing left to eat. I don't want to send them away hungry, or they will faint along the way."

Matthew 15:32

50 | Hey, I Love You, Jesus

Abba Father, today I want to simply tell you how much I love you. You have heard my prayers, so I don't need to ask you for that thing again today. You know my needs, and I am grateful. So let me tell you all the ways I am thankful for you. You are faithful. You are just. You lean in to hear what I have to say. You meet with me even when I am needy beyond belief, and you cheer me on as I grow in my understanding. I am at times a mess, but you still delight in my shaky steps of faith and obedience. What a friend I have in you. . . .

In any relationship, it is good and beautiful to tell them why you love them. What a sweet opportunity to do that today.

Sing psalms and hymns and spiritual songs to God with thankful hearts.

Colossians 3:16

51 | Wisdom

Lord, your Word says that if I need wisdom, you will give it to me generously. That means you will pour it out bigheartedly, openhandedly, liberally. I'm not going to refuse that offer. Help me to have wisdom in my closest relationships. Help me to lead with wisdom in all my decisions and choices. Pour out wisdom when I'm at a crossroads and I must make a choice that feels weighty. . . .

Clarify where you long for wisdom today. His offer to generously give you wisdom is not a one-time deal. It's there for you today, tomorrow, and when you need it next.

If you need wisdom, ask our generous God, and he will give it to you. He will not rebuke you for asking.

James 1:5

52 | Thank You

Holy Spirit, Jesus described you as a fighter. An Advocate. He said you know the heart of the Father regarding each of us, including me. Thank you for looking out for me. Thank you for having your best interests for me at heart. Thank you for those times you nudge me from the inside out when I'm about to take a wrong turn. Thank you for the peace I walk in, even when nothing around me is peaceful. Thank you that as I go out into this day I have an Advocate working on my behalf. . . .

Read Jesus' words in today's verse. Insert your name. Make that a prayer. How might that change the trajectory of this day?

And I will ask the Father, and he will give you another Advocate, who will never leave you.

John 14:16

53 | Shut It Down

Savior, you are not the author of condemnation. Shut down the voice of that inner critic that chatters away in my brain some days. It would like to be a constant companion, but it's not my friend. Truth is my ally. When that inner critic fires up, help me to confront it, for you have given me power to do just that. Help me to discern the difference between an inner critic and inner conviction. One is a bully and wants to shut me down. The other lifts me up. Today I will confront condemnation with concrete facts—I am growing in my faith, all God's plans for me are still yes and amen, and I am loved more than I can imagine. . . .

Who then will condemn us? No one—for Christ Jesus died for us and was raised to life for us, and he is sitting in the place of honor at God's right hand, pleading for us.

Romans 8:34

54 | This Is Who I Am

Jesus, those words hurt my heart. Those actions of another human brought pain. What I want to do is hide or fight back in anger. Help me to respond as a healed woman. A healed woman doesn't have to assume the burden of someone else's brokenness. A healed woman isn't required to receive every careless word. A healed woman knows that it is okay to share her need, or to gently ask that the conversation be turned in a new direction. A healed woman realizes there are times to love from a distance when someone is unhealthy or tries to discourage her in her faith. And most important, a healed woman understands that it is a power move to forgive. I place that person or those words in your hands, for you have insight I do not, and you love them deeply. Thank you for all the ways you've healed my heart and continue to make me whole. . . .

When Jesus saw her, he called her over and said, "Dear woman, you are healed of your sickness!"

Luke 13:12

55 | Today Is a Hard Day

Jesus, I'm weepy today. Hold my tears in your hands. Catch every one of them. I've needed to cry for a long time, and you are a safe place for them. I've held them back for so many reasons. I'm afraid if I begin, I won't stop. I've been so busy being strong for everyone else, I haven't given myself permission to let go. Tears feel vulnerable. Yet you wept, Savior. You stepped into those emotions and shared them with another. As I share my tears with you, I offer tears of sadness, tears of frustration, tears of joy, and tears of hope. . . .

Let the tears fall. Share with him what those tears represent.

Then Jesus wept.

John 11:35

Reflect on This

Not what I have, but what I have not, is the first point of contact, between my soul and God.

—Charles Spurgeon, *The Beatitudes*

56 | A Friend

Heavenly Father, I am asking today that you will bring me a friend. Someone who loves you authentically. I'm not asking for someone to fix me. Instead, I am asking for someone to simply connect with me. To fold clothes together or take a walk. To laugh. To drink a steaming cup of coffee. To cry. To pray together. You remind us that we are stronger together, Father, so give me the courage to reach out and meet someone new or forge a deeper relationship with someone in my circle. Thank you that I have something to offer her too. . . .

When life is challenging, it's easy to isolate. Take a moment and pray for a friend who is already in your life, or for that new friend who is just around the corner.

Share each other's burdens, and in this way obey the law of Christ.

Galatians 6:2

57 | In the Season of "No"

Lord, when things go the opposite of what I hope, you are still sovereign. You are still with me. I place my trust in you, for you have never failed me. You are with me in a season of waiting. You are with me in the season of "no." You are with me in the season of growth. You are with me when the clouds break and the sun shines through. That is where I place my hope and my heart. . . .

Your heavenly Father grieves with you. He weeps with you. He views you and this season with an eternal perspective. This is where we place our hope—in him who sees what we might not yet.

May your Kingdom come soon. May your will be done on earth, as it is in heaven.

Matthew 6:10

58 | My Source of Joy

Father, my joy is a little depleted, so I speak these things over my heart. You love me. You sent Jesus to earth for me. You planted the Holy Spirit in me so that I am never without direction. As I follow you, I am complete. I don't lack for anything—your Spirit is in me, over me, and goes before me. This Source of joy is ample enough to take me through this day. It is a deep well, not born of the world but born of my relationship with you as your daughter. I hold up this day and all that it holds, and I receive all the joy you want to give me as I go through it. Let it brim from the depths of my spirit and bubble up when I least expect it. Pour out your joy over me. . . .

I have told you these things so that you will be filled with my joy. Yes, your joy will overflow!

John 15:11

59 | Overwhelmed

Savior, I release all the things I cannot control and all the things I want to control. It's not that you don't have something for me to do in this hard place, but I am so busy scrambling and striving and trying to fix it all, I've become overwhelmed. So today I take a hard pause. Show me what is mine to control and what is not. Show me what is mine to do and what to put down. Thank you that there are times you just want me to rest. There are times you call my name and ask me to sit with you awhile. Thank you for each deep breath I take as I put it all down at your feet and listen for your voice. . . .

Ask God if there's something that needs to be put down. An unassigned task. A worry. Write it down. Take a deep breath—all the way in. Breathe out. Release the need to control that thing for even one more minute.

Anyone who believes in me may come and drink! For the Scriptures declare, "Rivers of living water will flow from his heart."

John 7:38

60 | A Prayer Just for You

This is my prayer over you today.—Suzie

Lord, thank you for revealing yourself to the woman holding
this book in her hands. You see her. You know her so well. You
are aware of how difficult all of this is and how brave she's
been. You've seen her when she's stood in a dark room with
tears. You've heard her when she's prayed for this season to end
and another to begin. Continue to reveal yourself as you meet
her in those places and in those questions. Show her that these
encounters with you are not by accident. They are not random.
They are purposeful. They are caring. They are powerful. Reveal
yourself to her one more time in this moment. Let her sense you
close. Wrap her in your love and assurance, in the powerful and
oh-so-beautiful name of Jesus, amen. . . .

I also tell you this: If two of you agree here on earth concerning
anything you ask, my Father in heaven will do it for you.

Matthew 18:19

Thankfulness Break

Father, I just want to begin this day with gratitude. Thank you for these seven things:

1. That last breath I just took

2. _____

3. _____

4. _____

5. _____

6. _____

7. _____

PART 3

Freedom in Hard Places

When hard pressed, I cried to the Lord; he brought me into a spacious place.

Psalm 118:5 NIV

61 | I Will Trust You

Almighty God, I have placed my trust in a lot of things. Yet there comes a moment when trust in you is our greatest asset. Today is that day for me. You survey the mountains and the valleys, and the obstacles ahead. You know the lay of the land, and where it is most beneficial to walk or run. You know the exact places where I can lie down and rest or fill up so I can continue on in this journey. You encounter principalities and powers and remind them that I am yours, and they must flee because it is you who stands between us. Lord, you cross the road before me. I take a step back to let you lead the way. . . .

As you talk to God about this, share with him where it's difficult to let him lead, and why. Thank him as you release that into his care.

But the Lord your God himself will cross over ahead of you.

Deuteronomy 31:3

62 | It's You

God, it would be easier if you did all the work and all I had to do was show up after, but that's not how you do it. You use regular people to do incredible works that reveal who you are. It's your strategy and it's beautiful—but can I be honest? It's also hard. I am highly aware of how embattled I feel and what I've faced these past few weeks or months or even years. It makes me wonder if people will look at me and say, "How could God use her?" Perhaps that's the miracle in all of it. If I were strong in my own right, they'd think it was all me. This way they can't help but know that you are what is making me strong. Thank you for helping me be strong and courageous. . . .

Being strong and courageous is placing your confidence in God rather than in your own might. What does God offer you that might be in short supply—in your own strength—right now?

Have I not commanded you? Be strong and courageous! Do not be terrified or dismayed (intimidated), for the LORD your God is with you wherever you go.

Joshua 1:9 AMP

63 | You're Still There

Lord, you are timeless. When this temporary season passes, you'll still be there. Your promises are not constrained by a day or a year. Your love is not diminished over time but stands true and firm. I can hold on to you because you will never disappear. You are not wishy-washy. Instead, when I wake up, you are there. When I dance in gladness, you are with me. When I fall to my knees, your presence covers me. When I cry, you see those tears. Even in the darkness, you are there. Your light takes me through the tunnel to the other side. You are constant, and that consistency is what I need. . . .

They will perish, but you remain forever. They will wear out like old clothing. You will fold them up like a cloak and discard them like old clothing. But you are always the same; you will live forever.

Hebrews 1:11–12

64 | I Praise You

Dear Jesus, praise is powerful. It shakes the heavens and it shakes the depths of hell. I am created to worship you, and it brings you joy. When I lift up your name, it not only resonates with you, it reminds me that I am your child. The words I say might not be fancy, but they are real. They come from the depth of my very being, and they shake the bonds of despondency. They rattle the enemy when he wants nothing more than to discourage me, and I'm all-out praising you. Praising you doesn't have to look a certain way. There's no formula to this. It's just the words of an embattled woman with a warrior's heart reaching up and out with worship. I love you, I love you, I love you. . . .

Worship isn't a formal act. It's personal. There's no perfect way to do it. There's no perfect place to do it. Yet when you speak it, those words reach the heights of heaven.

Around midnight Paul and Silas were praying and singing hymns to God, and the other prisoners were listening.

Acts 16:25

65 | Even Though

Abba Father,
Even though the fig trees have no blossoms,
and there are no grapes on the vines;
even though the olive crop fails,
and the fields lie empty and barren;
even though the flocks die in the fields,
and the cattle barns are empty,
yet I [*your name*] will rejoice in the LORD!
I will be joyful in the God of my salvation!
The Sovereign LORD is my strength!
He makes me as surefooted as a deer,
able to tread upon the heights.

Habakkuk 3:17–19

It's likely you don't have fig trees or an olive crop, but you do have a God who loves you like crazy. Rewrite this in your own words.

When Your Heart Is
Bummed Out, Burned Out

I felt as if I couldn't get enough rest. My mind was in overdrive pretty much all day and night. Things felt heavy, and that's unusual for this glass-half-full girl.

As I processed this with two friends, one said, "Suz, maybe it's burnout."

What, me? No.

The more I examined this, the more I realized that burnout isn't just about busyness. Burnout can be a state of emotional, physical, or spiritual exhaustion. You and I can be burned out from the weight of debates and painful discussions. We can burn out from trying to make sense of what is going on in the world, or in our own lives. We can be burned out from living in protective mode over those we love. We can be burned out from unexpected hardship or battles, and a multitude of other things. I don't know about you, but when I start to feel this way, I tend to hold up all the good things I've got going on—a family who loves me, good friends, a great church family.

It's almost as if I'm telling myself that I *shouldn't* feel this way, even though I do.

That thing you are feeling, it's real. Stop pushing it down. Stop listing all the reasons you shouldn't feel this way. Name it. Bring it to the light. This is a strong move.

When we give a name to how we feel, it removes the mystery. Maybe it's not burnout specifically, but we recognize that we are very close to empty in our emotional or spiritual tank. Like a red light on the dashboard of a car, it's clear we need to stop and refuel, but what do we do?

We often ignore it.

We keep going.

We continue to do what needs to be done.

While those things need our attention, refusing to refuel exacts a cost.

This is my prayer that came from a time like that.

Lord, I'm exhausted spiritually, emotionally, and physically. You know my heart. I want to point out why I shouldn't feel this way instead of acknowledging that I do. I've ignored your still, small voice calling me to slow down and refuel. Pour your Spirit over these tired spiritual bones and bring life to me one more time. But, Lord, I need to make a plan—a wise one. Will you help me do that?

Making a plan

As I took an honest appraisal, I realized I needed support. We tend to isolate when we are embattled. For me, the plan was to make a call to a couple of vibrant and life-giving friends. Meeting with them by Zoom or planning a coffee-shop date was just as important as all the other things on my calendar.

The second part of the plan was to assess my needs.

I hate to keep making car references, but just as each light on a dashboard reflects a specific need, it is important to clarify our own.

The next step is to be honest with those closest to us. When we share how we've been feeling and let them know what we need, it has the potential to make a big difference.

Your turn

If you are in that burned-out, bummed-out place, it just means you are human.

Name how you feel.

Bring it to the light.

Don't for one second beat yourself up about this. This is a strong and healthful move on your part.

Make a plan. It doesn't have to be extravagant. Maybe it's talking to a counselor. Perhaps it's a nap on Sunday afternoons. Maybe it's asking for help with a specific task or project.

Your needs are different from the person's next to you. So is your life. So make this personal.

Now, this is key: **Put those refueling to-do's on your calendar and honor them.** Filling back up is just as important as all the other things on the calendar. So many of us tend to put it on the calendar and then erase it when something else pops up.

When we honor that time, others start to honor it too.

As I took these steps, it took a little while to fill back up. That inner red light turned to yellow and eventually calmed down. I felt more rested inside and out. The optimist in me had never gone away, but she had a chance to breathe again.

If you feel bummed out and burned out, ask Jesus, the giver of life, to show you what you need in those burned-out places. Give yourself permission to stop pushing through so you can pause and be replenished. Stop making that list of why you *should* be grateful or why you *shouldn't* feel this way. God knows all of those things. He sees your heart. Instead, lean into the One who loves you, and then uncover the source of that burned-out, bummed-out feeling, for you are worth fighting for too.

Make Your Plan

What am I feeling?

What are my needs?

_____

_____

_____

What might that look like in practical terms?

_____

_____

_____

_____

Who is my support team? (Counselor, friends, church family, family)

_____

_____

_____

What is one step in my plan?

_____

_____

_____

_____

What is one thing I can put on the calendar for this week?

_____

_____

_____

_____

_____

66 | Living Water

God, you create streams in the desert. You take what is dry and parched and seemingly dead and bring it to life. Let your living water stream through me. Let it cover every dry place. Let it soak over every wilted dream. Spring up in the rocks that have stood in my way as I climb over them. I may be in the desert, but I am in the desert with the Creator and Sustainer of life at my side. I will not go thirsty or fade away under the hot sun. Instead, your living water will nourish me. It will bring new life and beauty where it seems impossible. I will not only make it through this season, but I will also come out on the other side of the desert filled to the brim with the Spirit of the living God. Take my eyes off the dry and dusty road I've been on and lead me to the stream one more time. . . .

When Jesus talked about living water in the New Testament, it was a fulfillment of this image of a stream in the desert. The Spirt of God is a flow of living water right where you are.

The parched ground will become a pool, and springs of water will satisfy the thirsty land. Marsh grass and reeds and rushes will flourish where desert jackals once lived.

Isaiah 35:7

67 | You Are My Rock

Heavenly Father, I will love you. I will consciously walk into your love and goodness. I will love you, for you are my Rock. I will love you as I find shade and rest under the sheer magnitude of who you are. I will love you as I climb into the crevices and caves of the massive fortress that is your name. I will love you as you shelter and protect me, and as you are my covering in the storm. I will love you as I find firm footing in my faith, for you are my Rock. I will love you as you hold me fast, even when it feels like I am tumbling in despair. I will love you because your character never changes, and I know what to expect even as everything else changes around me. I will love you, for you are a Rock for me. . . .

Tell the Lord all the ways you love him.

The LORD is my rock, my fortress, and my savior; my God is my rock, in whom I find protection. He is my shield, the power that saves me, and my place of safety.

Psalm 18:2

68 | My Wobbly Worship

O Lord, worship is so much more powerful than I realize. When I sing to you and it's off-key and wobbly, those words reach your ears and delight you. When I worship you in this hard season, the enemy's plans are thwarted. He wrings his hands as his tired, worn-out methods are unable to take me down in misery. David danced before you in the wilderness and it confounded those around him. I may feel shy about dancing before you, but my heart does not. It is full of gratitude. It is in awe of who you are. I may not have all the words to worship you, but I offer you my heart, my soul, my life, my everything. . . .

After consulting the people, the king appointed singers to walk ahead of the army, singing to the LORD and praising him for his holy splendor. This is what they sang: "Give thanks to the LORD; his faithful love endures forever!"

2 Chronicles 20:21

69 | Teach Me

Savior, you are making me new in this season. You are teaching me things that I can only learn through hardship. You are showing me how strong I really am. You are drawing me to a place of utter dependence on you. You are showing me how to listen for your voice. I'm like a seed planted in darkness. That seed may wonder if it will ever see the light, and yet in due time it is no longer hidden. It pushes through the soil and arises with newness and is complete and beautiful. Yes, I may be in a difficult season, but seeds of faith are growing in me. I will emerge as a strong woman anchored deep in my faith—because of you. Thank you for the new work you are doing inside of me even now. . . .

This means that anyone who belongs to Christ has become a new person. The old life is gone; a new life has begun!

2 Corinthians 5:17

70 | One Day

Jesus, when I think about heaven, it feels very far away, and yet I wonder . . . I wonder if you look at the years we have on earth and see them so differently than we do. For surely you see these years as a blink of an eye compared to eternity. I wonder if those who have gone before me are cheering me on even now. I wonder if one day when I stand before you, I'll look back and see this place of hardship the way you did, or if you'll take the veil from my eyes and I'll see how you carried me, how you loved me, how you protected me, and how you wept with me. Jesus, I'm thankful for the hope of eternity. I'm also thankful for this day. Either way, you are with me. . . .

Don't let your hearts be troubled. Trust in God, and trust also in me. There is more than enough room in my Father's home. If this were not so, would I have told you that I am going to prepare a place for you?

John 14:1–2

Word Picture Prayer

What is your favorite Bible story?

One of mine is the story of Jesus meeting Peter on the shore (John 21:7–17). It's just a handful of days after Peter betrayed Jesus and ran away in shame (Luke 22:54–62). Jesus is in his resurrected body and stands on the shore. Peter and the others are fishing, and Jesus calls out something like this . . .

"Catching anything?"

When they tell him no, he instructs them to throw their nets on the other side of the boat. They do and the nets are filled. This is so familiar to them.

Hadn't this same thing happened with Jesus?

One of the disciples cries out to Peter, "It's the Lord!"

When they reach shore, Jesus is quietly cooking fish over a campfire. Peter races to him. I imagine him stumbling onto the beach in astonishment. I also imagine the emotions he felt as he approached Jesus.

What will Jesus say?

Does he still love me?

How can I even be in his presence when I betrayed him?

Jesus not only welcomed Peter to sit with him around the fire, but he also took it a step further. He affirmed the love that Peter had for him, and he affirmed their relationship (John 21:17).

Praying a word picture prayer

One creative way to pray is to picture a story from Scripture such as this one. After all, these are real encounters with real people with real emotions and in real situations. If you have a loved one who has made a choice he or she regrets, this story of Jesus and Peter becomes a beautiful word picture. It unveils the character of Jesus and also demonstrates his love for those who fail or fall.

This story of Peter and Jesus can lead us into prayer over that loved one. It might look something like this:

Jesus, _____ made a choice they regret. They're ashamed and feel far from you. Yet I see who you are in this story as you interacted with Peter. You were merciful to him, and that same mercy extends to my loved one. Help them receive that mercy. Remind them that you long to welcome them back into community with you. Thank you that they have not gone so far that they are without hope. Thank you that you have more for them. Remind _____ of your love for them and of their love for you. Begin that restoration over their heart. Put them back on a path to peace and purpose. In Jesus' name.

Isn't this a powerful way to pray? Every prayer is heard by God. Yet a word picture prayer not only reaches his ears but bolsters your faith.

Now It's Your Turn

- Write the name of someone you care about who is on your heart, for any reason.

_____

_____

_____

- What is a favorite story about Jesus?

_____

_____

_____

_____

- Read that story in Scripture. Write down any words that describe the character of Jesus or ways he responded to that person within that story.

_____

_____

_____

_____

- Write a short prayer for your loved one.

_____

_____

_____

_____

71 | When I Am Impatient

Holy Spirit, I long to have the fruits of the Spirit evident in my life. Patience is not my strong suit. It's harder still when things are not going my way. Thank you for helping me. Instill patience over my thought life. Help it be a set of spiritual glasses as I view this trial through the eyes of my heavenly Father. Teach me to appreciate what is taking place inside of me as I trust you. In those times that I want to wrestle all of this into my own timeline, remind me that you are aware and are walking through this with me. I hold out my heart for this beautiful fruit of patience. . . .

Tell the Lord about those areas where you long for patience.

But the fruit of the Spirit is love, joy, peace, patience, kindness, goodness, faithfulness . . .

Galatians 5:22 ESV

72 | Laying It Down

Abba Father, my faith allows me to lay the whole weight of my circumstances down at the foot of the cross. This is where I find perfect peace. Whether my life is comfortable or in the trenches, my relationship with you holds me upright. And on those days when I do feel shaky, the door is open for me to sit and rest in your presence. Thank you for perfect peace—peace that brings harmony to the center of my soul even as my outward situation rages. Breathe your peace over me. . . .

Place your whole self in God's loving strength. What might you need to place at the foot of the cross?

You will keep in perfect peace all who trust in you, all whose thoughts are fixed on you!

Isaiah 26:3

73 | Finding My Rhythm

Holy Spirit, I know that my joy isn't tied to people or things. It's not based on my day, or my week, or what just happened five minutes ago. When the natural thing is to stamp my feet in frustration, you invite me to place my feet in a new direction—toward my faith. There I will discover what God has for me. There I find gladness. There is joy as my feet find rhythm with my heavenly Father. Thank you that joy is for me today. In this moment. For this time in my life. I say yes! Yes to joy. Yes to contentment from the inside out. Yes to moving forward rather than getting stuck. Yes to it all. . . .

In what ways are you saying yes to joy today? In what ways do you need to take your eyes off what is behind you to move forward? Share that with him.

And the disciples were filled with joy and with the Holy Spirit.

Acts 13:52 NIV

74 | I Am Not a Bother

God, I can't do this alone anymore . . . and yet I don't always ask for help, because I don't want to be a bother. I don't want people to think that I can't handle this on my own. The reality is everyone needs community, including me. Right now there are people who long to pray for me. There are people who have asked, "What can I do?" and I've not given them an answer. Maybe it's pride. Maybe it's that I'm used to being the one to come alongside others and this feels like new territory. Give me the courage to include those who love me in this battle. Help me to let down the wall and allow that person who loves me to come on in. . . .

What is one reason you may struggle with letting others come around you? Invite the Lord into that conversation.

Dear brothers and sisters, I urge you in the name of our Lord Jesus Christ to join in my struggle by praying to God for me. Do this because of your love for me, given to you by the Holy Spirit.

Romans 15:30

75 | Coming Close

God, there are a lot of ways to numb my pain, but you offer more than those things. You bring me to life. My pain becomes a backstory to my God story. As I look back, I see how many times you met me when I cried out. I see how I came out of that chapter of my life with your faithfulness etched on my heart. When I am tempted to numb, to hide, or to seek distraction so my pain will ebb, you don't condemn me for that but invite me to draw nearer to you instead. So, I'll do that right now, moving closer to you to simply sit in your presence. I don't have to know what to say. There are no expectations. I'm just putting my trust in you over anything or anyone else one more time. . . .

But as for me, how good it is to be near God! I have made the Sovereign Lord my shelter, and I will tell everyone about the wonderful things you do.

Psalm 73:28

Who Do I Have but You?

You guide me with your counsel, leading me to a glorious destiny. Whom have I in heaven but you? I desire you more than anything on earth. My health may fail, and my spirit may grow weak, but God remains the strength of my heart; he is mine forever.

Psalm 73:24–26

When the psalmist sang these words, he was in a perilous place, but he was also thankful.

Why?

He knew where to turn.

You remain the strength of my heart.

Because he believes this to be true, the psalmist knows the Source of his strength. The psalmist didn't see this as a one-time desperate cry for help, but an ongoing conversation. God is a shelter. He's present. On perilous days and on days when life is at ease. For a moment, I want you to imagine your heavenly Father as a shelter.

Doesn't that feel intimate?

Q: How might that change things, even in this moment?

76 | So Very Covered

Heavenly Father, while I have some understanding, it's hard to totally understand what God the Father, God the Son, God the Holy Spirit means in my faith walk. But I think it means I am completely covered. First, by you. Thank you for loving me so much. Thank you that you are greater. Thank you for seeing me, and for your touch upon my life. Thank you for your sovereignty. And Jesus! Healer. Encourager. Power in your name. Thank you, Jesus, for walking willingly to the cross for me, taking the burden of sin, and making us whole. And, Holy Spirit, who offers discernment, insight, wisdom. I'm so grateful that you lead me into truth when truth is hard to find. Because of this, who can stand against me when you are for me? What a powerful gift I've received from you. . . .

You are loved. You are rescued. You have a Helper. God is for you.

What shall we say about such wonderful things as these? If God is for us, who can ever be against us?

Romans 8:31

77 | Take My Anxious Thoughts

Heavenly Father, I am anxious. Thank you for allowing me to say that to you. You know that these are not worries about what might happen someday, but the experience of where I am. Thank you that you are my shield. Thank you that there is a reward in knowing you. I may be in the fire, but the flames don't consume me. I may be in a valley, but you lead me to living water. I may not feel peace about my situation, but your peace covers me. I may not know what tomorrow holds, but you allow me to find the miracle in today. Take my anxiousness and cup it in your hands. I trust you with every thought, every part of this day, every part of me. . . .

Write down that anxious thought. Ask God to help you hold it.

Some time later, the LORD spoke to Abram in a vision and said to him, "Do not be afraid, Abram, for I will protect you, and your reward will be great."

Genesis 15:1

78 | Holy Ground

God, when I come into your presence, it's holy. I may not see you, but you are there. I may not feel you in the beginning, but you long for me to wait until I do—even if it seems impossible. You see these meetings with you as holy ground, even if I'm in my kitchen or sitting on my back porch. Meeting with you becomes a transformative encounter, one that changes me. I may not know the "right" way to seek you, but I do know that you want to be found and that is what matters to you. So, here I am, showing up with a heart ready to encounter you all over again. . . .

A single day in your courts is better than a thousand anywhere else!

Psalm 84:10

79 | I'll Walk in Truth!

God, my heart can be influenced in a multitude of ways. That is why truth is so important right now. You are the greatest authority when it comes to what is true and what is not. When a lie tries to integrate itself into my day, I'll listen for your say-so. If I don't know what to believe, I'll come directly to you for answers. In that way, as well as a thousand others, you are my sanctuary. I can't help but be grateful, for you give me rest from burdensome half-truths and lies. More than that, you offer freedom. You remind me whose I am and where to turn. You lead me to truth that is liberating. . . .

What is one half-truth or lie that feels true? Go straight into the refuge of your relationship with God.

But as for me, I will sing of Your mighty strength *and* power; yes, I will sing joyfully of Your lovingkindness in the morning; for You have been my stronghold and a refuge in the day of my distress.

Psalm 59:16 AMP

80 | A Deep Well of Grace

Savior, I confess there are days I'm harsh with myself. I think of all the things I should be doing. I think of all the ways I should be stronger. I look at others and compare myself to them, when the truth is our battles are different. I wake up every day and do the best I know how. Change the way I am thinking. Redirect those thoughts that aren't helpful. When I set expectations impossibly high, remind me that you are merciful. Help me remember that you are a deep reservoir of wisdom and I don't have to figure this out all by myself. Draw me to peace. Draw me to restful thoughts. Help me stop wrestling and to hand you these temporary and troublesome thoughts. . . .

. . . let God transform you into a new person by changing the way you think.

Romans 12:2

Praying for a Friend

Once again, let's pause to consider if a name of a friend or even an acquaintance has come to mind this week. This is usually the work of the Holy Spirit.

- Write their name down in this space.

- Ask God to show you if there's something he wants you to do. That could be as simple as sending a text or dropping a handwritten card in the mail. It might be praying one of the prayer starters from this week and inserting his or her name in that prayer. Remember, God isn't asking you to shoulder the responsibility of fixing anything or anyone. Instead, he's inviting you to *partner* with him because that person is deeply loved and on his heart.

- What do you sense God leading you to do?

- Make a plan.

_____

_____

_____

- Share what you did here (and when).

_____

_____

_____

_____

When you come back to this page, follow up with them.

81 | This Day

Abba Father, though I count a lot of things, I don't often think about the number of days that I have here on this earth. I live as if I have forever, when that's not true for any of us. Every day is a gift, even those days that are difficult. Help me to see this day as a gift. Let me unfold it with gladness. I know that this day will contain challenges, but help me notice what is beautiful and good. Remind me to look around me and see your creation. Open my ears to hear that loving word from a friend or the laughter of a child. Help me not to rush through this day, as if it doesn't carry weight. Father, I'm slowing my pace just a bit to soak in the wisdom you have for me on this beautiful day. . . .

Slow down. What do you see? What do you hear? What miracle is right in front of you?

Teach us to realize the brevity of life, so that we may grow in wisdom.

Psalm 90:12

82 | So Much Hope

Savior, you call me to hope. This is a gift that comes as I walk with you. Hope is not limited by what I'm going through or even what is right in front of my eyes. Hope helps me to tune in to what you are doing on my behalf. Hope helps me search for you during this trial. Hope expands my view to include the eternal aspects as well as the day-to-day. Hope leads to patience as I wait. It keeps my feet moving forward when I want to plop on the ground and give up. And hope bathes my hurting heart, cracking open wide with a joy that no tongue can describe. Thank you for calling me to greater hope. . . .

Rejoice in our confident hope. Be patient in trouble, and keep on praying.

Romans 12:12

83 | Because of You

Jesus, I can do all things with your help. I just want to say that out loud as a reminder. When I am in the heat of the fight, it's easy to focus on how huge this all seems. It's easy to have temporary amnesia and forget all the times you showed up in the past. So, I'm going to look back. I'm going to speak out loud all the times you helped me be a faith warrior, not because of how skilled a fighter I was, but because you were in the ring with me. Yes, it was hard, and, yes, I received battle wounds as a result, but we made it through, you and I. . . .

Tell your Savior about a time that the fight was big and you felt small. Remind yourself of who he was as you faced it. Let it build your faith as you share these things together.

Think back on those early days when you first learned about Christ. Remember how you remained faithful even though it meant terrible suffering.

Hebrews 10:32

84 | Use My Story

Lord, you healed the sick. You shared good news with those who needed it desperately. You met with those who longed for a new way to live. Even on the cross, you saw a man who needed hope and you offered it. You said we would do even greater things than you. I don't fully understand that, but I believe that when you speak, it is truth. Maybe this means that when I join other believers around the world, that work goes further than we can imagine. We pray for others, or tell them about you, or sit with someone and share our faith story, and it reaches people around our home, our community, and around the world. Give me the courage to follow your lead. Thank you for letting me be a part of your beautiful work here on earth. . . .

We may think our most powerful ministry comes when times are good, yet there is nothing like sharing an "I understand." Pray that God will show you someone who needs prayer or encouragement. Pray for that one you've already met on your journey.

I tell you the truth, anyone who believes in me will do the same works I have done, and even greater works, because I am going to be with the Father.

John 14:12

85 | With You

Sovereign God, time with you over these past several weeks has drawn me closer to you. The difficulties I'm facing are genuine, but so is the fact that meeting with you makes me a warrior. I'm starting to understand not only the power of prayer, but the power of doing life with you daily. Those mountains still tower, but because of you, so does my strength to overcome them. With you, I can make it through anything. . . .

You are stronger than you know. Trusting God daily is the foundation of that strength. Look back today and see how much you've grown. Thank God for walking with you.

In your strength I can crush an army; with my God I can scale any wall.

Psalm 18:29

What Do You Need?

How can I help? Do you need anything?

When people ask these questions, we often meet them with "I'm okay. Thanks." The truth is we don't know exactly what we need, or we might struggle to answer because we don't want to be a bother.

Let's think about that for a moment. Let's flip it. What about that time you showed up for a friend in a crisis? Maybe you stocked her refrigerator with dinner for her and her family. Maybe you sat with her so she wouldn't be alone in a sterile hospital. Perhaps you rallied people to pray for her, or simply put your hand over hers and went straight to Jesus on her behalf.

That made a difference, but it also allowed you to be Jesus to her.

It's easier to give than it is to receive.

Yet we all have needs.

When I was a young mom, I needed a nap. Years later, when I was going through chemo, I needed a friend who saw me as Suzie and who would laugh with me, rather than worry about all the what-ifs.

What do you need right now, right where you are?

Who are the people who have said, "Hey, sis, I'd love to help"?

Answering these questions just may be the answer to your prayer—that one you prayed five minutes ago, or that one that's been on your lips each night. Let's look at that together.

What is one spiritual need (like prayer support)?

_____

What is one physical need (like a nap)?

_____

What is one emotional need (like coffee with a friend)?

What is one practical need (mowing the lawn, laundry, dinner)?

The next time a friend or loved one says, "How can I help?" share that need.

If there is someone you trust who has already asked to help, reach out to them.

Let that one do for you what you've done for so many others.

86 | There's No Other Way

Abba Father, I set my love upon you. I do this because I can't think of any other way to live. I may not feel it in every moment, but I know it. My love for you is deep in my spiritual bones. I'll choose to spend time with you and to listen for what you have to say to me. I'll find treasure in your Word. When I'm in the car or settling down for a breather, I'll think of you. Why? Because when I have called on you, you've heard me. Because you've been close by in my trouble. You've freed me, God, from the pressure of trying to think about what to say, and you've shown me that I can simply cry out to you and you know exactly what I'm saying. I love you, God, and I just want you to know. . . .

When they call on me, I will answer; I will be with them in trouble. I will rescue and honor them.

Psalm 91:15

87 | Me and You, Lord

Lord, this prayer connection with you has been sweet. I've learned how much I need it. Even when the hard places cease to exist, I will look for your light. Life is so up and down, but you are not. When I unite with you each day, I don't just find you. I find myself through you. I learn how dependence upon you bulks up my faith. Let's consider a time to talk every day. A time to grow. A time to sense you, know you, and be known by you. Thank you for bringing me through hard places in the past, and for meeting me again tomorrow. . . .

In your own words, tell Jesus why you love talking with him each day. Don't make this a pressure point or worry about a day missed. Tell him why you love connecting.

No longer will you need the sun to shine by day, nor the moon to give its light by night, for the LORD your God will be your everlasting light, and your God will be your glory.

Isaiah 60:19

88 | What I Want You to Know

O God, you have lifted me up and out. You have put my feet on solid ground. You've helped me crawl until I could walk. Walk until I could run. Run until I felt free. I may find myself crawling again tomorrow, but I'll know what to do. I'll get back up rather than stay down. I'll grab you by the hand as you steady me. I'll run with the wind in my hair and laughter in my heart. This hard place hasn't robbed me of my faith but solidified it. Thank you for all the times you've met me in the darkness when I didn't have a clue what to do. Thank you for all the times you've listened. . . .

Consider a "pit" where Jesus met you recently. What would you like to say to him about that moment?

He lifted me out of the pit of despair, out of the mud and the mire. He set my feet on solid ground and steadied me as I walked along.

Psalm 40:2

89 | Dancing Shoes

Jesus, let my feet dance again. One move, then another. My arms in the air. My soul lifted. Maybe in the shadows, or in the light I see in front of me. Rekindle my joy as I choose to see beyond today. Help me to celebrate every time you showed up, every time a messy miracle occurred, and every time I thought I was done and you reminded me my life and your plan for it were still ongoing. I am not defined by these past few weeks, or that event, or by that person. I am not consigned to live without hope. Instead, I'm a woman marked by a powerful Savior, and I'll dance in the darkness, and I'll dance in the light. That dance might be in my heart, or it might be in the privacy of my home. It might be in the words I speak to another, or the words I share only with you—but I will dance. . . .

This is who you are, friend. A faith-filled woman who isn't afraid to delight in her relationship with the Lord. Speak to joy. Ask for it. Step into it, right where you are.

Those who have been ransomed by the LORD will return. They will enter Jerusalem singing, crowned with everlasting joy. Sorrow and mourning will disappear, and they will be filled with joy and gladness.

Isaiah 35:10

90 | What I'm Learning

Lord, it's felt like forever at times, but you've been busy performing an incredible work in me. Hard soil was broken up and made smooth. Stones of anger and hopelessness and uncertainty were unearthed and removed. In their place, you've dug deep into my life and planted so many good things. Thank you! I've trusted you, leaned on you, cried out to you, hoped with you, and believed for a better tomorrow. I've also learned the power of appreciating what you have for me today, even in that hard place. Though I have been in this waiting season, it has not been idle.

What is sowed in sorrow is reaped in joy. I never understood that before, but I do now. If I have you, I have all I need. Thank you for walking with me through this, and for being there in all my days. I'm so grateful. . . .

Those who plant in tears will harvest with shouts of joy.

Psalm 126:5

Something Is Going On

> Then he said, "Don't be afraid, Daniel. Since the first day you began to pray for understanding and to humble yourself before your God, your request has been heard in heaven. I have come in answer to your prayer."
>
> Daniel 10:12

Daniel prayed for twenty-one days.

If you were to ask an observer what had taken place, they may have said *nothing*.

Yet Daniel continued to talk to God. Daily he showed up.

On the twenty-first day, an angel met Daniel and stripped back the veil between heaven and earth. What seemed like *nothing* was on one side of the veil. The other side revealed a battle zone. Darkness clashed with light. All of hell broke loose with the goal of discouraging Daniel, for the stakes were high. This man of faith wouldn't give up, so the enemy fought harder.

Daily he talked to God. Daily he showed up.

The moment Daniel began to commune with God, his request was heard.

The moment you began to commune with God, your request was heard. Take heart in that, friend. While it may look like *nothing* is taking place, don't discount what is happening beyond the veil. Your words reach the ears of heaven. God sees what is at stake. He sees beyond the obvious situation to the bigger picture, and cares about each. I think we'll be surprised one day when we stand before Jesus and that veil is gone. What might seem like words bouncing off the ceiling will be revealed as battlefields in the heavenlies. We'll see how those words or that time of prayer landed in eternity. We'll see the impact.

The Bible tells us that prayer is "powerful and effective" (James 5:16 NIV).

Don't underestimate what God has been doing these past few weeks. When it feels like nothing, remind yourself that something powerful is taking place.

Daily talk to God. Daily show up.

What Now?

Look Back

Take a few moments and go through a few of the prayer requests or needs you shared over the past few weeks.

If a prayer has been answered, note that.

Write down how God answered that prayer.

Celebrate it!

Tell someone about that answered prayer and encourage them too.

Scriptures to Encourage You

These verses were foundational to this prayer book. Select one to memorize or write on a sticky note where you can see it throughout the day for encouragement.

Care—Matthew 11:28; Isaiah 54:10; John 14:1–2; Psalm 116:2; Genesis 15:1; Psalm 91:15.

Confidence—Jeremiah 17:7–8; Psalm 56:4; Hebrews 13:8; 2 Corinthians 3:4–5; Philippians 1:6.

Direction—John 8:12; James 1:5; Joshua 1:9; Isaiah 60:19; Psalm 90:12; Psalm 18:29.

Faith—Jeremiah 17:7–8; Hebrews 12:1–2; Romans 15:13; John 10:10; 2 Chronicles 20:15; Luke 17:5–6; Psalm 51:12; Matthew 8:27; Romans 8:34.

Healing—Jeremiah 17:14; Matthew 15:31–32; Luke 13:12.

Help/Helper—Isaiah 41:10; Romans 8:26–27; John 14:16; Galatians 6:2; Joshua 1:9; Acts 13:52; Psalm 91:15.

Hope—Jeremiah 17:7–8; Psalm 56:4; Romans 15:13; Jeremiah 17:14; Ephesians 1:18–19; John 7:38; 2 Corinthians 5:17; John 14:12.

Joy—Romans 15:13; Psalm 51:12; Proverbs 31:25; John 15:11; Acts 15:31; Psalm 126:5; Isaiah 35:10.

Peace—Romans 15:13; Isaiah 54:10; John 14:1; Matthew 5:3–4; Isaiah 26:3.

Power—2 Corinthians 4:7–8; Ephesians 3:18; Colossians 1:11; Ephesians 6:11–13; Romans 8:31; John 14:12.

Prayer—Matthew 18:20; Ephesians 6:11–13; James 1:4–5; Matthew 18:19; Psalm 118:5; Psalm 116:2; Psalm 84:10; Daniel 10:12; Psalm 91:15; Romans 12:12.

Protection—Isaiah 43:2; Psalm 91:1; Nahum 1:7; Jeremiah 17:14; Daniel 6:21–22; 1 Samuel 23:14; Psalm 37:7; Mark 4:35–41; Deuteronomy 31:3; Joshua 1:9; Psalm 18:2; Romans 8:31; Psalm 59:16.

Rest—Psalm 91:1; Matthew 11:28; John 7:38; Psalm 118:5.

Restore—1 Peter 5:10; Philippians 1:6; Matthew 6:26; Isaiah 35:7; Psalm 40:2.

Strength—1 Corinthians 10:13; Isaiah 41:10; Ephesians 3:17–19; 1 Peter 5:10; Colossians 1:11; Philippians 4:13; Ephesians 6:11–13; Psalm 73:26.

Trust—Jeremiah 17:7–8; Psalm 56:4; Nahum 1:7; Galatians 6:9; James 1:4–5; Habakkuk 3:17–19; Psalm 18:2; Isaiah 26:3; Psalm 116:2.

How Prayer Starters Began

Years ago, I struggled to talk to God. I read books about prayer. I had a prayer checklist. I was taught formulas to help me pray. While there is merit in all of these, I longed to talk to God like a friend. I wanted to go deeper than a formula or a to-do list.

That's how prayer starters began. Daily I would read a passage of Scripture and study with pen in hand. I found myself talking to God, based on a story from Scripture or a thought. I'd talk to him about his character. I'd talk to him about a specific spiritual truth. Scripture helped me not only articulate how I felt but find hope and help. I did this as a young mom juggling everything, a young woman trying to find purpose, a follower of Jesus longing to hear from him so she could grow in her faith, and through hard places like cancer.

As I look back at those notebooks, I see the beauty of prayer starters.

I may not have known what to say, but Scripture showed me who he is and helped me begin the conversation. Later, I shared prayer starters with other women. The response was beautiful. One woman shared how a specific prayer starter helped her talk to God about things on her heart. Another talked about the wall that came tumbling down in her prayer life.

A friend I admired said, "Suzie, I've been practicing the prayer starters, and God and I are having conversations that are truly meaningful." She told me that even as someone who had been a believer for a long time, prayer often felt like a challenge. It was the one area of faith where she longed to be intimate, and yet she struggled.

That's what prompted this book. Thank you for joining in with women all over the world—whether you're new in your faith or a believer for a long time—as we begin a conversation with God, who loves us like crazy.

Thank you for being a part of this journey.

If you want to continue this journey, tune in to the Prayer Starters podcast, which airs five days a week. You can find it on your favorite podcast app or at klrc.com/podcasts.

Just for You: Creative Coloring Exercises

FROM THE MOMENT YOU FIRST
PRAYED GOD HEARD YOU

Our not enough becomes more than enough in His hands

GOD IS THE strength OF MY HEART and my PORTION Forever

Psalm 73:26

COME TO ME ALL WHO ARE heavy laden and I will give you Rest

MATT 11:28

God is the strength of my heart,
my portion forever.

Psalm 73:26b

Acknowledgments

Twenty years ago, I stood in a crowd of writers. I had mentally divided them into two camps. One, the writers, editors, and agents. Two, me, the wannabe. I had no idea what God had in mind, but I was willing. Twenty years and twelve books later I'm still in awe of following where Jesus leads.

Working with the team at Bethany House is a gift. My editor, Jeff Braun, is an encourager. I love how excited he gets about a new book idea. He loves what he does and that shows. Thank you, Jeff, for listening to me when I shared my heart for this book. Thank you for thinking outside the box with me. Thank you to the design and illustration and copyediting teams. Thank you for hearing my vision and running with it. Thank you, Bethany House team, for this beautiful partnership. I'll never forget the box that arrived at my doorstep when I was going through my own hard season. Such care went into that box—a soft blanket that I've used a hundred times, novels for this fiction-loving girl, chocolate (yum!), colored pencils, and beautifully illustrated inspirational coloring books.

I'm grateful to my husband, Richard. You've encouraged me for more than twenty years as I've run after my calling. You read my words. You are my greatest cheerleader, and you pray over me and the words I write. I'm grateful to my grown children and their spouses, all who love to celebrate with me when a book makes its way to the world.

And to you, the reader.

I love it when you send your thoughts. I love that many of you have become real-life friends. I love that we can grow in our faith together. Thanks for always showing up. Thanks for sharing my books with others.

You make this so fun!

About the Author

Suzanne (Suzie) Eller is the author of twelve books, including *Joy-Keeper*, *Come With Me*, *Spirit-Led Heart*, and others. She is a Bible teacher, speaker, and podcast cohost of *More Than Small Talk*. She is also the host of *Prayer Starters* on the KLRC podcast network. Suzie has been featured on hundreds of podcasts, as well as television and radio programs such as Focus on the Family, *Aspiring Women*, K-LOVE, and many others. She is wife to Richard, a mom, and Gaga to six children she refers to as a "joyful tsunami."

Suzie lives in beautiful northwest Arkansas. Her favorite things to do are hiking, kayaking, and finding the best food trucks.

Suzie is the founder of TogetHER Ministries. She loves coming alongside women to cheer them on in faith, to create connection, and to build community with women all over the world. She believes that healed women scoop up other women and run to the cross together.

Connect with Suzie

I love to hear from you. I delight in dropping in to say hello to small groups by Zoom. You can contact me through my website at tsuzanneeller.com. Here are some other places to connect!

- Website and blog: tsuzanneeller.com
- Facebook: facebook.com/SuzanneEller

- TogetHER FB community (a smaller, more interactive, and intimate community with four Bible studies a year and daily connection with Suzie): facebook.com/groups/suziestogethercommunity
- Instagram: instagram.com/Suzanne.Eller
- Pinterest: pinterest.com/suzieeller
- Twitter: twitter.com/SuzanneEller1
- Listen to *More Than Small Talk* (morethansmalltalk.com) on your favorite podcast app or at KLRC.com.
- Listen to *Prayer Starters* on your favorite podcast app or at KLRC.com.

More from Suzanne Eller

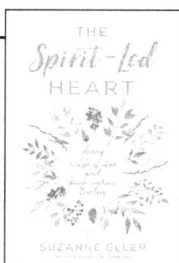

In her warm, vulnerable style, Suzanne Eller unpacks the promises Jesus shared with his disciples about the Holy Spirit, showing you how to stop settling for good enough and start truly living by his power. When you learn to unwrap the gift of his presence, you'll find the world-changing, soul-stirring life of passion and purpose God is waiting to give you.

The Spirit-Led Heart

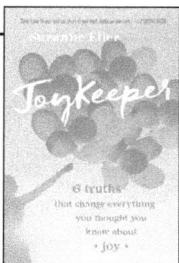

During a long season of sorrow, Suzanne Eller learned that in order to keep joy in her life, she needed to sort out her feelings and what she knew to be true. Examining six biblical truths, this book will help you see joy and God in a new light while offering thirty practical and inspirational daily exercises to intentionally practice these truths.

JoyKeeper

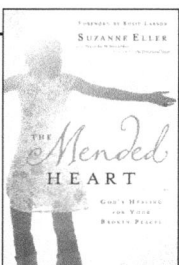

Popular author and speaker Suzanne Eller shows women how to embrace the powerful truth that Jesus has already completed the work that must be done to heal their brokenness, encouraging them to trust him, to give and receive grace, and to move ahead even stronger than before.

The Mended Heart

◊ BETHANYHOUSE

Stay up to date on your favorite books and authors with our free e-newsletters. Sign up today at bethanyhouse.com.

facebook.com/BHPnonfiction

@bethany_house

@bethany_house_nonfiction

You May Also Like . . .

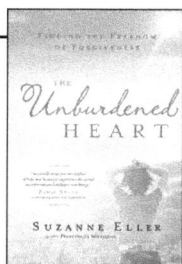

In this book, Suzanne Eller explores with readers the multiple facets of forgiveness found in Scripture, focusing in particular on the idea of leaving one place to go to another. Anyone can, with the help of God's Spirit, leave pain to find wholeness, leave regret to find purpose, and leave the past to live fully in the present.

The Unburdened Heart

www.ingramcontent.com/pod-product-compliance
Lightning Source LLC
Chambersburg PA
CBHW060752100426

42813CB00004B/788